DISSENT IN AMERICA

DISSENT
IN
AMERICA

by Robert A. Liston

McGraw-Hill Book Company
New York · St. Louis · San Francisco · Toronto

To Jack and Carol Paskins

Contents

Introduction

WHAT IS dissent? A popular dictionary defines "dissent" as disagreement or a difference of opinion. That is wide of the mark, however. Dissent involves something more than simple disagreement. Many people disagree on many subjects, yet are not in dissent.

Until quite recently, the word "dissent" was principally used in two areas, law and religion. In law, a dissent is a minority opinion by one or more members of a panel of judges. For example, a justice of the Supreme Court may write a dissenting opinion disagreeing with the majority of the nine-member court. In religion, dissenters were those members who broke away from an established church. Thus, the Pilgrims and Puritans who settled in America were dissenters from the Church of England.

Nowadays, the meaning of dissent has been broadened in newspapers and magazines and on radio and television

9

to refer to disagreement with the policies and practices of anyone in authority. Thus, people are said to dissent from the policies of federal, state, and local governments and their agencies, of schools and universities, of business and industrial enterprises, of political organizations, of various associations; and even from the attitudes of other people. Thus, various segments of the population are said to be in dissent with regard to such widely divergent matters as the war in Indochina, hair styles, length of skirts, attitudes toward women, university admission policies, the value of patriotism, and the dangers of smoking marijuana.

There is an element common to all expressions of dissent—*action*. For the purposes of this book, simply disagreeing with another person or a governmental policy does not qualify as dissent. The difference of opinion must lead to some *action* before dissent occurs. The Supreme Court justice takes action by expressing his views in a legal opinion which is published. The Puritans took action by leaving England and coming to the New World. Modern dissenters take action by attending meetings, circulating petitions, writing congressmen, marching in streets, battling police and national guardsmen—and burning buildings and setting off bombs.

This book is not a history of dissent in America. No effort will be made to trace in any orderly way the ideas which dissenters have expressed over the years.

Rather, this book might be called an investigation into dissent in the United States today. It endeavors to answer some questions. Are the forms of dissent different today and, if so, how are they different? Are the subjects of dissent different from those in the past and, if so, how are they different? What methods of dissent in the past have been most successful (and unsuccessful)? In other words, judging from the past, would a young person dissenting about educational policies achieve more effective results by circulating a petition, staging a strike, or blowing up the library?

I also hope to describe the methods used in the past by the members of the majority or established authority to repress or put down dissent and dissenters. Are the deaths of college students in Kent, Ohio, and Jackson, Mississippi, a new thing in America? Based on the past, what forms of opposition or repression are likely to be provoked by today's dissenters? Finally, I hope that a study of past dissenters will give some indication of what is likely to become of today's revolutionaries and their ideas.

It is customary to think of dissent in terms of radicalism, that is, some speedy, novel alteration of government, policies, or institutions. Past radicals have embraced socialism, communism, anarchism, and other "leftist" ideas. But dissent is not the exclusive property of radicals or "leftists." Reactionaries, those members of the far "right" who want no change or progress, dissent, too. In grandfather's day, the members of the Ku Klux Klan were just as much in dissent as the followers of the Socialist Party. Today, the Weathermen and the Minutemen may be poles apart in philosophy, but their violent expressions of dissent are nearly identical. This book will not deal exclusively with dissent from the Left or Right or any other political or social viewpoint.

In the preparation of this book I have been indebted to two individuals who provided invaluable research assistance: to Miss Marie Shaw and, particularly, to Tom Geismar, a student at Hiram College in Ohio. Thanks also go to Miss Thelma R. Bumbaugh, librarian at that college, who made pertinent books available to me.

Chapter 1
The Causes
of Dissent

THERE HAS BEEN a lot of dissent in America.

• • • In 1635, a rebel preacher named Roger Williams was banished from the Massachusetts Bay Colony by the Puritans because he opposed their harsh religious practices. Puritans customarily whipped, branded, mutilated, and even hanged individuals who disagreed with the Puritan religion or broke church rules. Williams fled into the wilderness to establish the colony of Rhode Island. This colony offered religious freedom to all, dealt fairly with the Indians, abolished imprisonment for debt and other harsh criminal punishments, and set up a truly democratic government based upon "the free and voluntary consent of all or the greater part of the free inhabitants."

• • • In the 1790s, farmers in Western Pennsylvania

rebelled against an excise tax imposed on whiskey. Because it was difficult to transport surplus corn over the Allegheny Mountains to Eastern markets, farmers made the corn into whiskey, which was easier to transport. In the Pennsylvania mountains there were as many as 5,000 distilleries in operation. To oppose the tax, farmers held mass meetings, agreed never to pay the tax, terrorized anyone who did pay the levy, and beat up tax collectors. To supress this "whiskey rebellion," President George Washington led 15,000 militiamen from four states into the region. The leaders fled and the rank and file quit. Two ringleaders were convicted of treason, but pardoned by Washington.

• • • In 1831, a mystically religious black slave named Nat Turner launched a revolt to win freedom for himself and other slaves. Turner and six other slaves, armed with scythes and axes, attacked the home of his master, Joseph Travis, killing the entire family. Turner marched to plantation after plantation, picking up followers as he went. During the march they killed fifty-seven whites. They were finally stopped in a pitched battle in which seventy-three black men were killed. Turner was captured and arrested six weeks later. He was hanged along with seventeen others.

• • • In 1892, workers at Andrew Carnegie's steel plant at Homestead, Pennsylvania, went on strike to protest a 25 percent cut in wages. To break the strike, Carnegie and his lieutenant, Henry Clay Frick, employed the Pinkerton Detective Agency to hire "scabs" or strikebreakers to work in the plant. When the scabs sought to

14

enter the plant by river barge, a pitched battle occurred with the strikers. The battle raged from early morning to five in the afternoon. There was much gunfire. The strikers even mounted a small brass cannon and fired on the Pinkertons. The artillery set fire to barrels of oil which turned the river into a fiery cauldron. The Pinkertons ran up a white flag and surrendered. Nine strikers and three Pinkertons were killed. About three times that many were wounded. The strike was ultimately broken when 8,000 National Guardsmen escorted the scabs into the plant. Dozens of strike leaders were arrested. Defeated, the men voted to return to work. In the aftermath of the strike, a man burst into Frick's office, pulled a gun and wounded him in the neck.

• • • On December 1, 1955, Mrs. Rosa Parks refused to "move to the rear" of the Cleveland Avenue bus in downtown Montgomery, Alabama. Hers was an individual protest against Montgomery "Jim Crow" laws requiring that black people sit in the rear of a bus, leaving the better front seats to whites. Police were called and Mrs. Parks was arrested. Thereupon, Montgomery's 17,000 Negroes organized a boycott of the bus line. Its leader was a 27-year-old clergyman named Dr. Martin Luther King, Jr. The boycott continued for 382 days, finally ending when the United States Supreme Court declared segregated seating on public conveyances to be unconstitutional.

• • • On a spring day in 1966, nineteen-year-old Barry Bondhus broke into the Selective Service office in Big Lake, Minnesota, and dumped two large bucketfuls of

15

human feces into a filing cabinet, thus mutilating the draft records of several hundred men who were about to be drafted for the War in Vietnam. He calmly awaited his arrest for destroying draft records. Convicted, he served eighteen months in a federal prison.

• • • In 1968, several hundred students barricaded themselves in a Columbia University building, holding a college official hostage for a time. Their act was a protest against the university's educational policies, its use of government funds to perform research aiding the war in Vietnam, and the university's decision to appropriate limited park space for the construction of a new gymnasium. The students held out in the college building for several days, raiding secret files, defacing records, breaking furniture and fixtures. New York City police using tear gas and swinging clubs finally dislodged them. Several students and police were injured.

• • • On June 23, 1970, more than 500 angry welfare mothers stormed the welfare department headquarters in Washington, D. C., demanding money to buy furniture. They smashed a heavy glass door, broke windows, tossed bricks, and scuffled with police who were called to evict them. Police arrested forty-four of the women. No one was seriously hurt.

These eight incidents, embracing almost the entire span of American history, were arbitrarily chosen from among many thousands of possible examples of dissent because they illustrate its variety.

What do religious persecution, taxation of whiskey,

16

slavery, a strike for higher wages, segregated seating on buses, the draft, university educational policies, and furniture for poor people have in common?

Another set of examples might have led to this question: *What do dumping tea in Boston Harbor, free public education, the founding of communities where property is owned in common, the eight-hour work day, lynchings, prayers in public school, long hair and love beads, and an impersonal, computerized society have in common?*

Do any characteristics unite such famous dissenters as Samuel Adams, the architect of the American Revolution, Thomas Jefferson, Andrew Jackson, abolitionists Frederick Douglass and William Lloyd Garrison, Susan B. Anthony, champion of women's suffrage, socialists and pacifists Eugene V. Debs and Norman Thomas, and Dr. King and Malcolm X, the two outstanding modern black leaders, with the host of young and less renowned people who are dissenting today?

There is an even more difficult question: do those welfare mothers, many of whom are black, have anything in common with the Ku Klux Klan, the organization which has used terror in an effort to enforce white supremacy for over a century? Do peace demonstrators who burn the American flag to protest the war in Indochina have anything in common with the "hardhats," the construction workers who scuffled with peace protestors and marched in defense of America and its flag?

To summarize, is there any common origin to the bewildering variety of dissent which has occurred and is occurring in the United States?

In the United States, the system of government virtually guarantees dissent. The democratic system probably cannot operate without it.

The first ten amendments to the Constitution, known as the Bill of Rights, made dissent the law of the land. These amendments guarantee freedom of religion and the press, peaceful assembly, and petition for "redress of grievances"; the right to bear arms; freedom from having troops quartered in a house without consent of the owner; freedom from searches and seizures without a warrant; freedom from testifying against oneself, from being deprived of life, liberty, or property without due process of law, and from being tried twice for the same crime; right to trial by jury, to confront witnesses, and to be represented by a lawyer both in criminal and civil cases; and freedom from the establishment of excessive bail in criminal offenses. The last two amendments reserve to the respective states or the people all powers not granted to the federal government.

The Bill of Rights gives any citizen of the United States a positive right to criticize the government or its actions orally or in writing. He can assemble peacefully for purposes of criticism. The existence of these rights assures that dissent will occur.

Dissent is further encouraged by the American system of government under which the majority rules and the winner takes all. There is no place in that system for a candidate defeated for office. When Richard M. Nixon was elected President in 1968, his opponent, Hubert H. Humphrey, a distinguished former Senator and Vice President, was immediately retired from public life. He could return only by seeking office again and winning.

And defeat, whether in seeking public office or in sponsoring legislation in Congress, can occur by as little as one vote.   Thus, the instant the majority rules on anything, it automatically creates a minority which is in disagreement or dissent.   Since that minority is guaranteed nearly full freedom to express its disagreement and to act upon it, the result has been nearly constant dissent in America. And nearly constant dissent has led to nearly constant efforts by the majority to enforce its rule, sometimes involving the use of police and troops.

Other factors have encouraged dissent, for instance the hundreds of years of unrestricted immigration, during which members of all races, religions, and nationalities came (or, as in the case of Negro slaves, were brought) to the United States.   With the immigrants came different languages and customs, as well as economic and political ideas.   Socialism, communism, and fascism are largely ideas imported into the United States, although fertile soil frequently existed for them here.

Dissent has been encouraged by the American economic system.   American capitalism helped create a large, generally prosperous middle class.   But until the last thirty-five years, American capitalism tended to create extremely wealthy owners of the means of production and large numbers of relatively poor workers and farmers.   This disparity between rich and poor was further enhanced by periodic economic depressions creating unemployment and poverty.   Thus, American workers for generations dissented from a system which prevented them from winning a larger share of the nation's wealth.

Until the last few decades, the sheer size of America

encouraged dissent. The United States always had a frontier, a new land to settle in the West where a man and his family could go in search of a better life. Resettling on the frontier was often an act of dissent against the previous conditions of life.

Thus, the American system of government, our economic system, and even the land itself have been causes of dissent.

Conscience, the personal sense of right and wrong and devotion to its dictates, has long been a cause of dissent. From Pilgrim to peace protestor, America has produced a small but influential minority which believes the individual must have a greater loyalty to *principle* than to other men, their governments, or their laws.

Perhaps the most influential statement of this view was made in 1849 by Henry Thoreau in his essay on *Civil Disobedience*.

> . . . when the power is once in the hands of the people, a majority are permitted . . . to . . . rule . . . not because they are most likely to be in the right, nor because this seems fairest to the minority, but because they are physically the strongest. But a government in which the majority rule in all cases cannot be based on justice, even as far as men understand it. Can there not be a government in which majorities do not virtually decide right and wrong, but conscience?—in which majorities decide only those questions to which the rule of expediency is applicable? Must the citizen ever for a moment, or in the least degree, resign his conscience to the legislator? Why has every man a conscience, then? I think we should be men first, and subjects afterward. It is not

desirable to cultivate a respect for the law, so much as for the right. The only obligation which I have a right to assume is to do at any time that which I think is right.

Thoreau believed that every man had a positive right, indeed a duty, to refuse to obey laws or in any way encourage government acts which were wrong. Man should not fight in unjust wars, pay taxes used in unjust causes, indeed, do anything which in conscience he deemed wrong. Thoreau went to jail rather than pay taxes to support the Mexican War or the continuation of slavery, which he believed were the chief wrongs of his time.

If a thousand men were not to pay their tax bills this year, that would not be a violent and bloody measure, as it would be to pay them, and enable the State to commit violence and shed innocent blood. This is, in fact, the definition of a peaceable revolution, if any such is possible . . . When the subject has refused allegiance, and the officer has resigned his office, then the revolution is accomplished. But even suppose blood should flow. Is there not a sort of blood shed when the conscience is wounded? Through this wound a man's real manhood and immortality flow out, and he bleeds to an everlasting death. I see this blood flowing now.

Thoreau's statements have ringing force:

Cast your whole vote, not a strip of paper merely, but your whole influence. A minority is powerless while it conforms to the majority; it is not even a minority then; but it is irresistible when it clogs by its whole weight.

Under a government which imprisons any unjustly, the true place for a just man is also a prison.

The biggest cause of dissent, however, lies in the words written by Thomas Jefferson for the Declaration of Independence. "All men are created equal and endowed by their Creator with certain inalienable rights of life, liberty and the pursuit of happiness." Those words were an expression of the aspirations of many of the colonists who had settled the New World. Those words have rung through history as an expression of what is frequently called the "American Dream." As Americans, both individually and in groups, have sought to fulfill their interpretation of the meaning of those words, they have encouraged a bewildering variety of dissent.

Interpretation is the vital word. The hardhats and the peace protesters, the welfare mothers and the Klu Klux Klan (KKK), are each working toward their own interpretation of the American dream. Those people who were involved in the whiskey rebellion, who marched with Nat Turner, who struck for higher wages, who refused to move to the rear of the bus, who defaced draft records or seized university buildings were all—admittedly in widely disparate forms—protesting what they considered some form of injustice. It is this protest against injustice in the effort to fulfill one particular interpretation of the American dream which links all who dissent in America.

It may be possible to fulfill the American dream of equality and human rights, but successive generations of

Americans have never quite succeeded. It has not been for want of trying.

Consider voting, which Americans consider vital to the democratic process. Universal suffrage has always been part of the American dream, yet we have never quite achieved it. The voters who were mentioned in the Constitution were basically men of property. In 1800, Thomas Jefferson was swept into office after campaigning to extend the vote to farmers and workers. A generation later Andrew Jackson was voted into office after large numbers of poor and less educated men in the West received the vote.

After the Civil War, the Constitution was amended to give the vote to Negroes. This was circumvented by terrorism and restrictive state laws imposing property, ancestral, and literary tests upon black people. In 1920, after generations of effort, American women received the right to vote. Beginning in 1962, the United States Supreme Court reached a series of decisions requiring that members of Congress and state legislatures represent approximately equal numbers of people. This effort was called the principle of "one man, one vote." In 1965, Congress passed the Voting Rights Act, which attempts to insure—at long last—the vote to black citizens.

It is painfully obvious that despite repeated efforts, America has not yet reached universal suffrage.

And there are other examples. When the United States was founded, child labor was taken for granted. Workmen toiled under such appalling conditions and for such little wages that a major source of argument before the

Civil War was whether the lot of the Negro slave in the South or the "wage slave" in the North was worse. A strong case could be made for both.

The efforts of American workmen to achieve shorter working hours, better working conditions, and higher pay form a major segment of American history. It is a story filled with violence, bloodshed, and suffering.

Workingmen achieved a large measure of victory in the 1930s and 1940s under the "New Deal" administration of Franklin D. Roosevelt. Laws were passed recognizing the authority of labor unions and insuring their power in contests with business and industry. Yet, strikes still occur. New dimensions of the labor problem are just emerging in strikes by government employees such as transit workers, garbage collectors, and postal employees and in efforts by Negro workers to win membership in white unions so they, too, can get better jobs.

Thus, despite great effort and considerable progress, America has still not achieved peace in labor relations, decided what constitutes a fair division of national wealth, or afforded equal opportunity to all people who want to work.

People today are usually familiar with the efforts of Negroes, women, and Indians to achieve equality throughout history. They may be less familiar with the battle which has been waged for better education. In the early decades of American history, the creation of a system of free public schools was a major victory of the reform movement. Ever since, demands have continued for better buildings, better teachers, better books, more facilities.

Today, high school and college students are fighting for educational reform. The American dream in education is still far from fulfillment.

There is one other major portion of the American dream which has long been a cause of dissent—peace. There are those who would argue that Americans are not really a peaceloving people; we only think we are. After all, the United States in less than 200 years has been embroiled in nine "Wars"—Revolutionary, 1812, Mexican, Civil, Spanish-American, World Wars I and II, Korean, and Vietnamese. In addition, there were the long wars against the American Indians and military escapades in the Philippines, Nicaragua, Cuba, Dominican Republic, Tunisia, Lebanon, and several other places. American military personnel are today stationed over much of the world. Indeed, a strong case can be made that Americans are not peaceloving and are being hypocritical when they say so.

An equally strong case can be made the other way. Until the end of World War II, in 1945, America never maintained a strong peacetime military establishment. Prior to that, America always disarmed after every war. The Army and Navy were impoverished in peacetime. Indeed, America found it difficult to raise an army in every war up to World War I, when there was a more equitable draft. In every previous war, military commanders were plagued by inadequate manpower, short enlistments, and desertions. It may be said that Americans have elected a significant number of generals as President, from Washington to Eisenhower, but they were not elected because they were military men but because their wartime accomplishments had made them popular and respected. Indeed, it was Eisenhower, a career soldier, who warned America about the dangers of the military-industrial complex, thus raising an issue for dissenters ever since.

The best evidence that peace is part of the American dream lies in the opposition, the dissent to American wars. Every war but one has met with determined dissent. The exception is World War II. The United States had been attacked at Pearl Harbor and Americans viewed Nazi Germany as an unmitigated evil which had to be destroyed.

The story of dissent in American wars is a book in itself. Fortunately, historians are beginning to write about it, thus correcting one of the common inaccuracies in American histories. American wars were hardly a unanimous outburst of patriotic fervor. In the American Revolution, a small band of revolutionaries turned dissatisfactions and British blunders into the War for Independence. All during the war large numbers of people remained loyal to the King and opposed to the war.

Many individuals considered the War of 1812 unnecessary, and many others believed it was immoral to fight Britain on the side of the dictator Napoleon. New England leaders met in Hartford, Connecticut, to consider secession from the Union.

The Mexican War was greeted with a torrent of opposition from people who felt it was monstrously immoral to steal land from Mexico which would be used to extend slavery.

26

Opposition to the Civil War was so great in the North that President Lincoln had to use harsh methods of repression. More than 13,000 people were jailed and more than twenty newspapers were shut down. Restrictions were placed on assembly, speech, press, and the right to speedy trial. There were several major riots in which troops had to be used to restore order. The opposition to the war was based on the belief that it was immoral for brother to kill brother and that there were other ways to settle the conflict.

The Spanish-American War was so short that the dissent never had much time to make itself known. But dissenters were appalled when the United States seized the Philippine Islands from Spain and sent in troops to quell an uprising by Filipinos who wanted independence. The charge of immorality was heard again.

World War I was opposed particularly by Socialists such as Eugene V. Debs and people of Germanic descent. Congress, at the urging of President Woodrow Wilson, passed Espionage Acts aimed at repressing dissent. Many hundreds were arrested under these acts, which in effect suspended the Bill of Rights.

The Korean War encountered much dissent, particularly from people who felt it was being run rather stupidly. There had been opposition to entering the war at all. On the other hand, many Americans, perhaps a majority, disagreed with the concept of a limited war to maintain independence for South Korea, and felt, like General Douglas MacArthur, that China and North Korea should be defeated in an all-out war.

This brief description of a few of the major areas of

dissent in America leads one to the conclusion that the American Revolution has never quite ended. What the nation's founders fought and died for, as expressed by Thomas Jefferson, has never been fulfilled. In one form or another, for one reason or another, each successive generation of Americans has produced people who have taken up the battle, dissenting and dissenting and dissenting to nudge the American majority closer to the dream of life, liberty, and the pursuit of happiness. Today's young dissenters are following in a long tradition.

Dissenters, moreover, have ultimately succeeded, in many cases, in winning the majority to their point of view. To use a popular expression, we've "come a long way, baby" since 1789. At no point has perfection been achieved, but the vote has been extended, workers have shorter hours and higher pay, black people have greater freedom and opportunity, and the quality of American education is better. We do not have peace, but the striving for it is undiminished.

Chapter 2
Dissent
by Revolution

THE BOMB and the gun, dynamite and the bullet. There are those in America today who see these as the best, indeed, the only way to change the political and economic system of the United States.

One expression of this came from Joe Harris, a black student from New York City writing in the book *The High School Revolutionaries:*

> Military power is the power of the gun, the fire bomb, the tank, etc. This is the power that must be taken by the people. Since the people have no land and no money, they are left with no choice but to get guns, cut the strangulating, parasitic hold of America by the capitalists and set up a decentralized government that is truly of the people and by all the people. To be truly a government of the people, it must be socialist, with the people controlling the means of production. To stop the exploi-

tation, the oppression, and the fascism that exists in America today, the people must grasp the power of the gun to overthrow the oppressor.*

A similar expression came from an unidentified man who admitted that he had been involved in bombings. His statement appeared in the April 13, 1970 issue of *Life:*

> We are revolutionaries, not reformists.   We're not trying to frighten the Establishment, we are trying to destroy it, so that a just society can be built based on human values, not on financial or commercial values.   It's necessary to have a real struggle of some kind before people will listen and reconsider their concept of what America is.   Ours is an attempt to attack capitalism, racism, exploitation—directly and militarily.**

Many others might be quoted, including the Weathermen, a militant left group of the Students for a Democratic Society.   They took credit for several bombings in 1969 and 1970, including one in the New York City Police Headquarters.   An explosion in a town house in Greenwich Village in New York in 1970 killed at least three youths who had been making bombs there.   In November, 1969, three large office buildings in New York were rocked with bombs.   Other explosions, apparently for revolutionary purposes, occured in the state of Cali-

* Reprinted by permission of Random House, New York, from the book *The High School Revolutionaries,* edited by Marc Libarle and Tom Seligson. Copyright 1970.
***Ibid.*

fornia, Colorado, Washington, Maryland, and Michigan.

Today's revolutionaries, that is, those people who would overthrow the American political and economic system by force of arms, come from a long line of distinguished forebears. The United States is the oldest continuous democracy in the world. During the nearly 200 years of its existence, it has withstood a great many armed rebellions and attempted revolutions. In many of them, the methods of revolt were identical.

The first major rebellion was led by Nathaniel Bacon in Virginia in 1676. His family was one of the wealthiest and most important in England. He was a cousin to the wife of Sir William Berkeley, the aged colonial governor of Virginia. When Bacon arrived in Virginia, he was welcomed as a member of the ruling clique. He promptly purchased two large plantations.

Despite his origins and wealth, Bacon's sympathies were with the common man. "The poverty of the country," Bacon said, "is such that all the power and sway is got into the hands of the rich, who by extortious advantages, having the common people in their debt, have always curbed and oppressed them in all manner of ways."

Bacon assumed leadership of the disgruntled farmers and laborers. Agitating in the legislature, he managed to have some reforms enacted. But they were not enough. A direct confrontation with Berkeley led to Bacon's being declared a "rebel." Thereupon, on June 23, 1676, he led 500 men into Jamestown, the capital, and drove out the Governor and his cronies. They took refuge on the eastern shore of Virginia across the Chesapeake Bay, while Bacon

31

took control of the colony and instituted numerous reforms.

Berkeley raised an army and drove Bacon and his men from Jamestown. Before Bacon could reopen the battle, he died of dysentery. Without his leadership, the rebellion collapsed. Bacon's leading supporters were rounded up and thirty-seven of them were executed.

As a revolution, Bacon's Rebellion was a failure, yet it accomplished much. Many of his reforms were maintained.

Almost a century later, in the 1760s, the frontier settlements, or "back country," of North and South Carolina erupted in revolt. The basic cause, aside from grinding poverty, was the government's neglect of the area. In South Carolina, back country people had virtually no protection from harassing bands of outlaws and Indians. The settlers of western South Carolina set up a vigilante government, and created their own courts to try outlaws. The vigilantes swore allegiance to each other and coined a name for their organization, the Regulators. The state assembly—a man had to own 500 acres and twenty slaves to qualify for membership—eventually set up six circuit courts in the back country, but the South Carolina Regulators remained active well into the War for Independence.

In North Carolina in the late 1760s, the situation was somewhat different. The problem was not lack of government but bad government. Frontiersmen were plagued by unequal taxation, extortion by judges and sheriffs, uncertain land titles with many foreclosures of farms, high interest rates, and other forms of greed. The settlers of five western counties banded together and called themselves Regulators. They sought to redress their grievances by refusing to pay taxes and by assaulting colonial officials. Governor Tryon sent in militia to put down the revolt. On May 16, 1771, a force of 2,000 Regulators confronted half that many militiamen. In the Battle of the Alamance River, the poorly armed and undisciplined Regulators were routed. Nine were killed on both sides. Fifteen Regulators were captured and tried. Six were hanged. Governor Tryon and his army made a triumphal tour through the back country extracting an oath of allegiance from every male citizen. But not all were present to give it. Many Regulators fled to Tennessee to found that state.

Victory in the War for Independence did not stop armed revolts. After the war, the fledgling nation was plunged into a severe depression. Unemployment was high. Little money was circulated. Production was at a low level. Many war veterans returned home to find themselves with staggering debts and nothing to pay them with. Some states tried to relieve these conditions by printing paper money, issuing it to veterans in sums equal to their debts. Creditors often went into hiding rather than accept these nearly worthless "greenbacks." In states where greenbacks could be used for all forms of payment, storekeepers closed their doors.

In Massachusetts, however, the highly conservative legislature refused to issue paper money. They insisted that debts be paid in "hard" currency at the full value. With high unemployment and little money in circulation, Massachusetts courts began to foreclose on farms. Land, buildings, cattle, and even furniture were seized and sold for debts.

In western Massachusetts, the farmers revolted under the somewhat reluctant leadership of Daniel Shays, a bankrupt war veteran. On August 29, 1786, he led 500 men armed with clubs and muskets to prevent the Common Pleas Court in Northampton, where debtors were tried, from sitting. Another group closed the court at Great Barrington and broke open the jails to release debtors. In September, Shays marched to Springfield and tried to place his men in front of the Supreme Court building, determined to stop the foreclosures and force the state legislature to issue paper money. Shays' men were met by a contingent of state militia. Shays agreed to withdraw on condition the court adjourn.

On January 25, 1787, Shays, leading 1,200 men, tried to seize the Springfield Arsenal with its large supply of guns and ammunition. Militia armed with cannon met his force. With the first volley, the rebels broke and ran. The militia pursued Shays' Army and on February 4, defeated it in a battle in the snow at Petersham. Shays escaped, but fourteen leaders were captured and sentenced to death. All, however, were pardoned or let off with short prison terms.

Shays' Rebellion was not a total failure. The state legislature did amend the laws to allow veterans' notes to be tendered in lieu of taxes. The public became aware of the need for a strong central government. The Constitutional Convention was convened the next year. A sidelight of the rebellion was a comment from Thomas Jefferson, who was then American minister to France. From Paris he wrote:

A little rebellion now and then is a good thing; the tree of liberty must be refreshed from time to time with the blood of patriots and tyrants.

Slavery spurred revolt. One man who saw force and violence as the only way to end slavery was Gabriel, a slave on the plantation of Thomas Prosser in Henrico County near Richmond, Virginia. In 1800, Gabriel was a twenty-four-year-old coachman, a job that gave him a chance to travel throughout the area. He was over six feet tall and heavily built. He affected long hair, as had his Biblical hero, Samson. Like Samson, Gabriel wanted to use his strength to pull down the evil temple of slavery.

He proposed to lead about 1,000 slaves to attack the state of Virginia at its weakest link, the city of Richmond. It had a population of 40,000 but only about 8,000 of these were white. He would march on Richmond at night, seize the poorly defended arsenal, break out the weapons, and march throughout the state, killing all slaveholders and persons who approved of slavery. The rest of Virginia's 347,000 slaves—nearly half the total population —would follow his banner and he would set up an independent black state.

During the summer of 1800, Gabriel recruited his followers in secret. Weapons were fashioned: stones, clubs, swords made from scythes, crude spears. A few rifles and bullets were stolen.

On August 31, the revolutionaries were to meet in Old

Brook Swamp about six miles outside of Richmond, then march into the city in three columns. Surprise would be their greatest weapon. First, the arsenal, then, Richmond, finally all of Virginia would be theirs.

They never marched. A violent storm arose. Rain fell in a deluge, washing out bridges. The rebels could not find their way to the swamp, let alone to Richmond.

The attack was postponed. Two slaves reported the conspiracy to their master. Within hours the state militia—all white—was called out and a detachment of federal cavalry sent to protect Richmond. Without surprise, Gabriel's plan had no chance of success.

White Virginians went on a rampage of repression. Slaves were rounded up whether or not they had been involved in Gabriel's plan. "Trials" were held and sentences imposed. Some slaves were beaten, thrown into chains or sold out of the state. Thirty-four were hanged, including Gabriel. At his trial he is believed to have uttered these words:

> I have nothing more to offer than what General Washington would have had to offer, had he been taken by the British and put to trial by them. I have adventured my life in endeavoring to obtain the liberty of my countrymen, and am a willing sacrifice to their cause; and I beg, as a favor, that I may be immediately led to execution. I know that you have pre-determined to shed my blood, why then all this mockery of a trial?

There were two other major slave revolts, one led by Denmark Vesey in 1822 and the other by Nat Turner in 1831.

Unlike the white rebellions the slave revolts produced no reforms. Their chief effect was to tighten the shackles of slavery on the black man. Harsh laws were passed preventing assembly and travel of slaves. The South took elaborate measures which successfully prevented any future large-scale revolts.

In 1842, Thomas W. Dorr organized and led a rebellion in Rhode Island. That state had departed so far from the principles of its founder, Roger Williams, that it disfranchised half its citizens through property qualifications. Dorr and his followers marched in large parades demanding free suffrage. Their slogans harked back to the American Revolution: "No taxation without representation" and "Liberty or Revolution."

When the propertied voters refused to heed their demands, they organized a rump convention and drafted a "People's Constitution." In 1842, Dorr called his own elections in opposition to the official slate. Two separate governments emerged, each claiming to be the official one. Dorr was declared in rebellion and martial law was instituted. Dorr led his followers in a raid on the state arsenal, but they were defeated by the militia. Dorr was arrested and sentenced to life imprisonment at hard labor. The following year a more liberal state constitution was adopted.

John Brown, a tall man, gaunt, humorless, deeply religious, and a fanatical abolitionist, spent years trying to destroy slavery—but not with talk. "What is needed is action," he said, "—action!"

His concept of action was violence, forcibly wresting the slaves from their masters, freeing them, and killing all who stood in his way. He prepared for this by studying military strategy, learning the tactics of guerilla warfare, and poring over maps.

He first struck in Kansas in 1856. The people of the Kansas Territory were to decide whether the state would be slave or free when it was admitted to the Union. Partisans on each side poured into the state, determined to influence the outcome. Brown and five of his sons—he had twenty children by two wives—went to Kansas determined to make it a free state.

His first act was the Pottawatomie Massacre. With four of his sons and three others he entered the pro-slavery village early on a Sunday morning, awakened five people from their beds and killed them as an example to slavers. In retribution two of Brown's children who had not taken part in the massacre were killed. Brown helped to launch other raids. He fought several pitched battles against larger forces, but usually won, for he was an expert in military tactics. Finally, at Osawatomie, he and forty others were defeated by a group of 250 slavers. Ill, Brown had to leave Kansas, but the warfare he had launched continued in "Bleeding Kansas" until the Civil War.

Brown returned east from Kansas, now determined to carry out his grandiose plan to free the slaves. He would capture the federal arsenal at Harpers Ferry, Virginia, arm nearby Negroes, and march into the South. He would not stop until every black man was liberated.

With a group of sixteen white men (including two of his sons) and five Negroes, Brown captured the arsenal on October 16, 1859. Several prominent citizens were taken as hostages. The Virginia militia and federal troops under Colonel Robert E. Lee quickly poured into the area. The arsenal was surrounded. Brown and his men knocked holes in the brick walls and fought the troops. The battle went on for two days, but Brown was defeated. His two sons and eight others were dead. Others fled, but Brown and four of his companions were arrested.

Within a week Brown was tried and sentenced to death. His words before sentence was pronounced bore the ring of the revolutionary:

> Had I so interfered in behalf of the rich, the powerful, the intelligent, the so-called great . . . it would have been all right. Every man in this court would have deemed it an act worthy of reward rather than punishment. . . . I believe that to have interfered as I have done, in behalf of His despised poor, I did no wrong, but right. Now, if it is deemed necessary that I should forfeit my life for the furtherance of the ends of justice, and mingle blood further with the blood of my children and with the blood of millions in this slave country whose rights are disregarded by wicked, cruel and unjust enactments, I say, let it be done. . . .

Brown's bloodshed at Harper's Ferry served to galvanize feelings that led directly to the Civil War. Abolitionists saw him as a martyr. Many agreed that only force would end slavery. The pro-slavery forces in the South saw Brown as an example of what the North would do to end slavery. They determined to use force to prevent it.

The Civil War was the greatest single act of dissent in United States history. Eleven southern states (Virginia,

39

South Carolina, North Carolina, Georgia, Florida, Alabama, Mississippi, Louisiana, Texas, Arkansas, and Tennessee) left the Union and set up the independent Confederate States of America. The reasons for the dissent were to maintain slavery and state's rights and to protect Southern interests from the growing industrial might of the North. The result of the rebellion in the South was a four-year war in which the South was defeated militarily and forced back into the Union.

As a revolution the secession was peculiar. For one thing, it was a revolution of conservatives. The world's major revolutions, those in America, France, and Russia originated on the Left among people who wished to change the economic and political system. The Southern secessionists were anything but "leftist." They were conservatives who wished to maintain the status quo. They wanted to continue the economic condition (slavery). They did not want to change the political system. In fact, they adopted a political system amazingly similar to the one they had just left.

Nor was the rebellion the particular work of revolutionaries. True, there had been talk of secession for many years. But no organized band of conspirators schemed to secede from the Union. Rather, secession was the nearly spontaneous reaction of Southerners against what they considered intolerable pressures and abuse from the North.

Overwhelming military force and economic strangulation ended the Confederacy. Forced back into the Union, Southerners began to use non-revolutionary means of achieving the same goals. The Negro was freed only nominally. Restrictive state laws and social pressures (along with terrorism) were used to keep him in a state close to slavery. Southern politicians were returned to Congress repeatedly until, under the seniority system, they held great power. For over one hundred years the Southern politician kept the Federal government at bay, leaving the South to run itself as it wished.

No United States revolutionaries were stranger than the "Molly Maguires" of the 1860s and 1870s. They were anthracite coal miners in Pennsylvania, where tens of thousands of Irishmen worked in semi-darkness, knee-deep in water. About one-fourth of the workers were children aged seven to sixteen, who were paid one to three dollars a week to separate coal from slate. Adults were paid on various formulas, but by whatever method their pay came to about eleven or twelve dollars a week. To earn even this pittance, the Irish miners worked from dawn to dusk under the most brutalizing conditions.

At that, they were lucky if they lived to work, for mine accidents made the miners an extremely poor insurance risk. On September 6, 1869, 175 miners died in a fire in Luzerne County. o They had been trapped because the mine operators had failed to build a safety exit. One accounting showed that in Schuylkill County alone 556 miners were killed and 1,655 injured in one seven-year period. Following a mine accident, a leader of a labor union told his men:

Men, if you must die with your boots on, die for your families, your homes, your country, but do not longer consent to die like rats in a trap for those who have no more interest in you than in the pick you dig with.

During the 1840s and 1850s, the miners tried to effect reforms through unions, but this failed. Mine operators imported strikebreakers. State troopers and special police always prevailed over the miners.

Beginning about 1860, the miners began to resort to terrorism. Most of the Irishmen belonged to the Ancient Order of Hibernians, an organization intended to "promote friendship, unity, and true Christian charity among the members." A member of the Order who had a grievance against a boss took the matter before a committee which met secretly in a home or tavern. If the committee concurred, an appropriate punishment was decided upon, such as threatening, beating, or killing the offender. Members of an order in another town were assigned the task of carrying out the punishment. This made detection more difficult. Over the years, violence of one form or another was visited upon mine foremen and superintendents, strikebreakers, and even occasional union leaders whom the miners felt had betrayed them. It must be said that most of the punishments were threats. A person would receive a crude picture of a coffin and a warning to leave town immediately. Many intended victims took the warning.

A hostile press dubbed the Irish miners the "Molly Maguires." Molly had been a woman in Ireland in the 1840s who carried pistols under her petticoat. She used the guns to dissuade landlords and baliffs from evicting tenants. Her assassinations made parts of Ireland uninhabitable to all but her followers.

The Mollies' terror tactics continued for about fifteen years. All efforts to smash them were unsuccessful because they were a secret organization more loyal to themselves than to any outsiders. Finally, in 1873, Franklin P. Gowen, leader of the coal operators, hired the Pinkerton detective agency to smash the Mollies and paid the agency $100,000 for the job. Pinkerton sent a young agent named James McParlan to infiltrate the Mollies. As Irish as the men in the mines, he was initiated into the Order in April, 1874. The following year the miners went on strike to protest a cut in wages. The strike dragged on for six months. The miners subsisted for days on bread and water. At the same time Gowen organized his own band of terrorists known as the Modocs. Along with mine police, the Modocs beat and killed union leaders. The Mollies reacted with intensified terrorist tactics. The anthracite coal region was filled with bloodshed.

Ultimately, hunger prevailed and the miners were forced to return to work at a 20 percent cut in pay. Soon afterwards, McParlan began informing on the Mollies. He claimed knowledge of murders and attempted murders. Scores of Mollies were arrested and tried. Nineteen were sentenced to death and many others received long prison sentences. The trials were hardly a high point in American jurisprudence. Gowen had himself named prosecutor at many of the trials. McParlan was the principal witness at each trial, along with miners who had been accused of crimes but escaped prosecution by turning state's evidence. The wife of one of the witnesses claimed that her own husband rather than the accused had committed the murder. But evidence was not as important in the trials as the desire to "get" the Mollies. The arrests and trials were successful. The Mollies never recovered from the loss of their leadership.

One of the most celebrated and climactic experiments with revolution occurred in Chicago in the 1880s. Long a hotbed of radicalism in the United States, Chicago seethed with revolutionary ideas. Socialism was one. Workers, many of them immigrants from Europe, believed that only through national ownership of the means of production could the workingman receive his fair share of the nation's wealth. Such an economic system was the goal of the Socialist Labor Party. It aimed to organize and persuade workers to vote for socialism in the United States.

But the ballot box was too slow a process for a minority of the socialists in Chicago. In dissent from the dissenters, they sought to "accomplish by force what they could not obtain by the ballot." As early as 1875 armed bands called Educational and Defense Societies were formed. These paramilitary groups grew in size and soon formed Revolutionary Clubs outside the Socialist Labor Party. In 1881, these far left groups held a convention from which came the Revolutionary Socialist Labor Party. Its platform advocated the formation of labor unions along "communistic" principles. The ballot was ridiculed as "an invention of the bourgeoisie to fool the workers."

These revolutionaries were called "anarchists." An

anarchist is usually a person who is against all forms of government because they interfere with individual liberty. The Chicago "anarchists" were not against all forms of government. They had a program for government—socialism. Because they were popularly known as anarchists, the dictionary today contains a second definition of "anarchist": a person who uses terror as a form of resistance to organized government.

In 1882, the Chicago anarchists received a big boost with the immigration of Johann Most from Europe. A native of Germany, Most had been treated cruelly as a child. An operation had permanently deformed his face. Hatred and violence were almost instinctive to him. As a young man he was converted to socialism. He had a spectacular career in Germany, Austria, and England, serving terms both in jail and in the German parliament. In both places he was a bombastic advocate of violence to overthrow capitalist governments. When Alexander II, the czar of Russia, was assassinated in 1881, Most published an article praising the murder and urging others to copy it. For this he was jailed in Britain. Upon his release he came to the United States.

He went on a speaking tour of principal American cities and his oratory recruited many people to anarchism. In 1883, anarchists from twenty-six cities joined to form the International Working People's Association. Its manifesto stated:

We could show by scores of illustrations that all attempts in the past to reform this monstrous system by peaceable means, such as the ballot, have been futile, and all such efforts in the future must necessarily be so. . . . Since we must then rely upon the kindness of our masters for whatever redress we have, and knowing from them no good may be expected, there remains but one recourse—FORCE!

Johann Most not only talked revolution, he wrote it. He published a pamphlet entitled *Science of Revolutionary Warfare—A Manual of Instruction in the Use and Production of Nitroglycerine, Dynamite, Gun-Cotton, Fulminating Mercury, Bombs, Fuses, Poison, Etc., Etc.* On April 8, 1885, he wrote:

Here is something worth hearing. A number of strikers in Quincy yesterday fired upon their bosses, and not upon the scabs. This is recommended most emphatically for imitation.

A month later, *Die Arbeiter Zeitung,* a German language newsapaper published in Chicago, urged: "Workmen, arm yourself!" Another article in the newspaper was as follows:

Dynamite! Of all the good stuff, that is the stuff! Stuff several pounds of this sublime stuff into an inch pipe (gas or water pipe), plug up both ends, insert a cap with a fuse attached, place this in the immediate vicinity of a lot of rich loafers who live by the sweat of other people's brows, and light the fuse. A most cheerful and gratifying result will follow. . . .

46

All of this was mostly talk and very little action. The spark that changed things came on May 3, 1886 with a strike at the McCormick Harvester plant in Chicago. A strike had been going on there for three months, when 300 strikebreakers guarded by 350 police entered the plant. The strikers held a mass meeting near the plant. During the meeting, the plant whistle blew and the strikebreakers started to leave. A riot immediately began with the strikers pelting the scabs with stones and fists. Police opened fire. Four men were killed and many wounded.

The anarchists reacted with fury. *Die Arbeiter Zeitung* ran the headline: "BLOOD! Lead and Powder as a Cure for Dissatisfied Workers—This is Law and Order!" A handbill was circulated reading: "Revenge! Workingmen, to arms!!!"

A protest meeting was held the next day, May 4, in Haymarket Square in Chicago. About 3,000 men, women, and children showed up to listen to a succession of speeches by leading socialists such as August Spies and Albert Parsons. But the speeches were relatively mild and the protest was quite tame. The Chicago mayor circulated among the crowd and decided "nothing is likely to occur to require interference."

Late in the afternoon a light rain began to fall and all but 500 of the protesters went home. Socialist Samuel Fielden was on the verge of sending the rest of the crowd home when a police inspector ordered 176 policemen to break up the gathering. A police captain, sword drawn, shouted: "I command you in the name of the people to immediately and peaceably disperse." Fielden replied, "We *are* peaceful."

47

At this point a bomb went off near the police detachment. In the panic which followed police began shooting indiscriminately, at each other as well as at protesters. Within two or three minutes, seven policemen were dead and 67 wounded. Casualties among the demonstrators were two or three times as great.

No one ever discovered who threw the bomb. Various theories were put forth: an anarchist had thrown it; the police had done it deliberately to provoke a riot; someone else had sought to settle a score with the police on a matter entirely unrelated to anarchism or socialism.

Identification of the bomber did not matter. Chicago police went on a rampage. Hundreds of Chicago workers were arrested. Homes were searched. Meeting halls and printing shops were invaded at will. It went on for weeks with attendant newspaper publicity, for each time homes were entered rifles, ammunition, and anarchist pamphlets were found. There were a number of bombings of anarchist offices. These were attributed to the anarchists. But there is evidence that the police themselves did much of the bombing and planted material to be "found" by searchers, all in an effort to destroy the anarchist movement. In a newspaper interview three years after Haymarket, the Chicago police chief said:

It was my policy to quiet matters down as soon as possible after the 4th of May. . . . On the other hand, Capt. Schaack [a Chicago police officer] wanted to keep things stirring. He wanted bombs to be found here, there, all around, everywhere. . . . After we got the anarchist societies broken up, Schaack wanted to send out men to organize new societies right away.

Two weeks after Haymarket, ten men were arrested and charged with murdering a policeman during the riot. Of the ten, one escaped and another turned state's evidence. The remaining eight included Spies, Parsons, Fielden, and other leaders of the anarchist movement. It was virtually impossible to prove the murder charge against them. No one knew who had thrown the bomb. Moreover, only Fielden had been physically present at Haymarket when the bomb exploded. Instead, they were accused of provoking the murder by their inflammatory speeches and articles. In his summation to the jury, the prosecutor said:

> Law is on trial. Anarchy is on trial. These men have been selected, picked out by the grand jury and indicted because they were leaders. They are no more guilty than the thousands who follow them. Gentlemen of the jury: convict these men, make examples of them, hang them and you save our institutions, our society.

All eight were convicted and seven sentenced to hanging. Eventually four were hanged, the rest sentenced to long prison terms. The trial was denounced as a travesty of justice around the world, but it broke the back of anarchism in America.

Other, more recent disturbances have been called revolution, rebellion, or insurrection. Notable examples were the urban riots of the 1960s. In scores of cities, including Los Angeles, Newark, Detroit, Cleveland, New York, Baltimore, Washington, and Chicago, black ghettos erupted into rioting, burning, and looting. There was sometimes sniper fire. Police were overwhelmed. National Guards and even federal troops had to be enlisted to restore an uneasy peace. Dozens were killed and hundreds injured. Property damage ran to hundreds of millions of dollars.

These riots were in many ways similar to rebellions, yet it is difficult to ascribe such a word to them. There was very little evidence that the riots were any form of conspiracy, that is, planned by a person or group of persons for a specific date. Most studies have shown that the riots were a spontaneous outpouring of the pent-up fury and frustration of ghetto residents against poverty, discrimination, and futility. By burning stores and homes and attacking police, they openly expressed their hatred for white control of their communities and for the arrogance of police. The riots destroyed large areas of the ghettos and worsened the housing and employment conditions of the residents. On the other hand, they did lead to some reforms and an increase in governmental efforts to aid ghetto people.

What can be concluded from the history of rebellion in America? What can today's advocate of revolution discover from the past?

It is painfully obvious that the use of force and violence to effect change leads to overwhelming counterforce and violence. All attempts to overthrow the American political and economic system or to change it through violence have been met with whatever governmental and military force was necessary to quell them.

The nature of the counterforce has been fairly consistent. Police, state militias, and federal troops have been used frequently to put down rebellion or violent dissent. Private citizens, vigilantes, and special hired detectives have been employed. The use of the police informer to infiltrate the revolutionary group is quite old in America. The arrest, trial, and elimination by death or imprisonment of the leaders of the rebellion has been used consistently. Only occasionally have the acts of violence led to governmental reforms which alleviated the cause of the violence.

Today's revolutionaries are using methods startlingly similar to those of their forefathers. Today's revolutionaries form organizations, some of them secret, plan revolutions, hold rallies and protest-marches, arm themselves, advocate force as the only way to change America, and use the counterforce employed against them as a means of "radicalizing" the moderate or disinterested. As in the past, today's violent dissenters use inflammatory speeches and writings, rocks, bricks, guns, and bombs. Seizing buildings, taking hostages, issuing demands for reforms, burning and pillaging property are as much yesterday's methods of revolution as today's.

There are striking similarities, too, in the counterforce used to quell revolution, whether actual or advocated. The elimination of revolutionary leaders or violent dissenters goes on today. The FBI, as well as the police, has infiltrated such groups as the Communist Party, the Ku

Klux Klan, and the various organizations of campus radicals. This has led to arrests and trials. The Black Panther Party, which advocates a program of violence to change the American system, contends American police are carrying on a systematic program to eliminate its leaders by arrest or death. Whether or not this is true, many of the Panther leaders have been killed, jailed under high bonds, or forced to leave the country.

The similarities between the past and present also extend to the motives for violence and rebellion. These include dissatisfaction with American life; a desire to do away with the capitalist system and introduce socialism or communism; dislike for corruption and privilege in the United States; and hatred for police and the violent measures they sometimes employ.

Does the long history of broken rebellions and repressed violence mean that current efforts are hopeless? Not necessarily. Repeated outbreaks of violence and the consistent suppression of it certainly could lead many people to conclude that violent revolution in the United States is folly. But a confirmed revolutionary might point out that the history of the world's major revolutions shows that success came after repeated failures. For example, the Russian czars managed to crush many revolutions before the Bolsheviks succeeded in 1917.

Chapter 3
Peaceful Dissent—
Violent Repression

PEACEFUL, NON-VIOLENT PROTEST, has often been met with determined, even savage repression. This is a particularly unappetizing phenomenon of American dissent.

In 1877, America was mired in one of its cyclical depressions marked by high unemployment, reduced wages, shortage of money, and much suffering. On the afternoon of July 16 of that year, forty brakemen and firemen of the Baltimore & Ohio Railroad went on strike at Camden junction near Baltimore. It was an unorganized protest against a 10 percent cut in wages. And it was a peaceful protest.

The forty Maryland strikers were soon joined by other workers. The strike spread from coast to coast and confronted the United States with its first nationwide strike.

The strike spread to Martinsburg, West Virginia, where 1,200 B&O workers struck. When the mayor and police arrested the strike leaders, miners and other workers joined the strike. They gathered into a crowd and released the arrested men. Governor Matthews, answering the railroad's request, sent in the state militia. There was a confrontation on July 17 and shots were fired. A striker was wounded. Angry workingmen and their sympathizers staged another demonstration. At this point, two companies of militia went over to the strikers' side, refusing to shoot. Governor Matthews appealed to President Rutherford B. Hayes for federal troops. They were sent immediately. Strike leaders were arrested and the strike was broken in Martinsburg.

It then began to spread. When soldiers marched on the railroad station in Baltimore to entrain for Cumberland, they were met by thousands of workers. In the battle which followed, twelve men were killed and eighteen wounded.

The strike spread to other railroad lines. In Pittsburgh, workers of the Pennsylvania and the New York Central Railroads struck and were joined by a variety of other workers and unemployed men. On July 21, assembled strikers were ordered to disperse. When militiamen were sent in to disperse them, they refused to fire. To contain the situation, the state governor sent in militia from far-off Philadelphia. They were met by a large crowd which hissed and booed them. The soldiers opened fire, killing twenty and wounding twenty-nine The New York *Herald* reported:

The sight presented after the soldiers ceased firing was sickening. Old men and boys . . . lay writhing in the agonies of death, while numbers of children were killed outright. Yellowside, the neighborhood of the scene of the conflict, was actually dotted with the dead and dying; while weeping women, cursing loudly and deeply the instruments which had made them widows, were clinging to the bleeding corpses.

The *Herald* quoted a soldier, "I served in the War of the Rebellion and I have seen wild fighting . . . but a night of terror such as last night I never witnessed before and hope to God I never will again." A grand jury later called the act "an unauthorized, willful and wanton killing . . . which the inquest can call by no other name than murder."

In reaction, the strikers turned violent, indiscriminately burning boxcars and railroad buildings. Five million dollars in equipment was destroyed.

Still the strike and the killing went on. Thirteen were killed and twenty wounded in Reading, Pennsylvania. A member of President Hayes' cabinet suggested that Pennsylvania be declared in rebellion.

In Chicago, tens of thousands of workers left their jobs, paralyzing the entire transport system of the Midwest. On July 24, police, cavalry, and strikers met in a bitter battle on Halsted Street. As many as 20,000 men were involved. Perhaps fifty separate mobs were fighting, attacking residences and destroying railroad equipment. At least thirty were killed and almost one hundred wounded. When the strike reached St. Louis, a general strike was called and the city closed up tight. Only massive use of police, militia, and federal troops brought order. There were mass arrests, leading to imprisonment and fines.

Hundreds of strikes in this period led to violence. One of the worst was the Pullman strike of 1894. It was the nation's first *organized* nationwide strike.

The Pullman Company manufactured railroad sleeping cars. It employed about 6,000 workers in its plant at Pullman, Illinois, near Chicago. The workers were compelled to live in the town of Pullman, owned by the company. They paid rent to the company, bought at the company store, and abided by rules set forth by George M. Pullman, head of the company.

In the spring of 1894, Pullman laid off more than 2,000 workers and cut wages from 25 to 40 percent. But no reduction was made in prices in the company store or in company rents, which were 25 percent higher than in nearby Chicago.

The Pullman workers were members of the American Railway Union, ARU, a new labor organization headed by Eugene V. Debs. In April the local union membership struck Pullman. For three months the strike was a local affair. In June, the ARU organized a boycott of Pullman cars. Most, though not all, railway workers across the country refused to move trains that contained a Pullman sleeping car. As many as 125,000 railroad workers were involved in the boycott. When the railroad operators refused to detach the Pullman cars, the railroad workers went on strike.

The railroad industry, organized into the General Managers' Association, fought the strike by traditional methods, importing scabs and firing workers. At this point, it was nationwide but still a fairly typical labor strike.

Debs, a pacifist, constantly exhorted his men to avoid violence. If they simply stayed off the job, they would win.

Into this situation the United States Government trod with a heavy foot. The United States Attorney General at that time was Richard B. Olney, a former railroad lawyer, director of several rail companies, and a member of the General Managers' Association. He determined to break the strike. First, he went to court and obtained an unprecedented injunction. The strike was forbidden. All union leaders were forbidden to take any action on behalf of the strike, including disseminating information about it. The injunction was used to jail workers who refused to return to work.

President Grover Cleveland, on the advice of Olney, called out state and federal troops. This action was supposedly justified because the strike interfered with the movement of mail, even though strikers had scrupulously permitted all mail trains to operate. Eventually, troops appeared in twenty states.

Violence followed. On July 5, in Chicago, a railway signal house was destroyed and railroad tracks blocked. Regular soldiers made a bayonet charge into the workers, wounding several. The next day $340,000 worth of railroad property was burned. There was rioting. A bystander was shot by a policeman one hundred yards from the scene of a riot. When the wounded man tried to rise, he was shot dead. On July 7, a crowd attempted to stop the moving of a train by the National Guard. Guns fired and twenty persons were killed.

With an estimated 14,000 troops in Chicago, the situation remained tense for several days. President Cleveland issued a proclamation against the right of assembly in eight states, including Illinois and California. Newspapers fanned the tension with such headlines as: ANARCHISTS AND SOCIALISTS SAID TO BE PLANNING THE DESTRUCTION AND LOOTING OF THE TREASURY. Labor leaders were joining together, however, to call a nationwide general strike. The nation appeared to be on the point of rebellion. Two men were instrumental in preventing it, Samuel Gompers, head of the American Federation of Labor (AFL), and Debs. Gompers was in sympathy with the strike but hesitated to take action that could lead to revolution. Debs was willing to end the strike to stop the violence. By August 2 the strike was over. It was a massive defeat for labor. The ARU was destroyed. Debs and other leaders were jailed.

The Pullman Strike of 1894 was an instance of peaceful dissent which turned to violence when the heavy hand of repression occurred.

This pattern has been repeated hundreds of times. In his book *Radicalism in America* Sidney Lens makes this statement:

> Time and again workers in mass production industries and on the nation's railroads were driven to violence on a scale far outstripping anything in Europe. No country in the world has witnessed so many picket line battles and so many deaths on picket lines as the United States. Figures are fragmentary to document this point, but a

survey made by *Outlook* magazine in 1904 gives some idea of how extensive was this phenomenon. In the thirty-three months prior to the survey—not a particularly exceptional period—198 men were killed in picket lines in thirty states, 1,966 injured, 6,114 arrested.*

Still the repression and the killing went on. In 1905, a strike by teamsters resulted in the death of twenty and injury to 400. In 1903–4, a strike by miners at Cripple Creek, Colorado, resulted in forty-two deaths, 112 wounded, 1,345 imprisoned for months without trial and the forcible deportation of 773. In 1914, workers in Ludlow, Colorado, struck the Colorado Fuel and Iron Company, owned by John D. Rockefeller. Evicted from their company-owned dwellings, the strikers moved into tents. To protect their families, the strikers built a cave inside the largest tent. Thirteen children and a pregnant woman were housed there. On Easter night, company police and national guardsmen poured oil on the tents and set fire to them. The woman and children perished in the conflagration, along with six others sprayed with gunfire.

This sort of violence studded the labor movement throughout the 1920s and 1930s. Not until the 1940s, after passage of federal laws protecting the rights of labor organizations, did the strike cease to be an invitation to violence. Many strikes have occurred since 1940, some quite large and serious. Police still appear at strikes, but

* Reprinted by permission of Thomas Y. Crowell Company, New York, from the book *Radicalism in America* by Sidney Lens, copyright 1966.

they are there to keep order and protect the pickets.

But it took over a century for the United States to allow peaceful dissent by workers to proceed without threats of violence from police and soldiers. The open warfare of the picket line may seem part of the distant past to American workers today, yet it is not too distant —nor is it unrelated to dissent today.

American Negroes, as a dissenting minority, have been subjected to violent repression. The sit-in phase of the Negro revolution in the 1950s and 1960s is an example of violent repression of peaceful dissent.

Leaders such as Dr. Martin Luther King, Jr., James Farmer, Stokely Carmichael and Roy Wilkins constantly preached non-violence. The demonstrators themselves were trained in techniques of non-violence, trained that is, to endure insults and even physical attacks without retaliating. And the aim of the demonstrations was peaceful. The protesters sought to integrate schools, restaurants, hotels, theaters, parks, and other public places. They sought the right to vote, to live where they wished, to hold jobs. By marching through the streets, praying and singing, by sitting in restaurants and by other peaceful means, they called attention to the segregated plight of the Negro. By being arrested for "trespassing" or "disorderly conduct," they sought to challenge the legality of the state and federal laws requiring racial segregation and denying the vote, housing, and employment to black people.

In city after city this dissent was met with repression. Scores, sometimes hundreds of demonstrators were arrested, thrown bodily into police vehicles, and put behind bars for varying periods of time.

In April and May, Dr. King led a major effort to integrate Birmingham, Alabama. Day after day Dr. King led non-violent marches, only to be met by police who sprayed the marchers with firehoses. Police dogs and mounted police were used. At least three bombs were exploded in the Negro ghetto of the city. One demolished the home of Dr. King's brother, the Rev. A. D. King. Another rocked the headquarters of the Negro integrationist movement. Finally, on September 15, a bomb exploded in a church, killing four young girls attending a Bible class and injuring scores of other youngsters. Two other youths were shot and killed that day.

In 1965, Negroes marched in protest against discrimination in Negro voter registrations in Selma, Alabama. During five days of demonstrations, sheriff's deputies charged the marchers on horseback, flailing them with nightsticks and whips. Scores were injured. More than 3,000 were arrested. There was one death, Mrs. Viola Liuzzo, who was shot while running an automobile shuttle service during the march. Three members of the Ku Klux Klan were convicted of conspiracy in her murder.

Repression of peaceful dissent has not been confined to workingmen and Negroes. In 1932, about 20,000 World War I veterans formed the "Bonus Expeditionary Force" and encamped in Washington, D. C., demanding immediate payment of veterans' bonuses. The payments were due in 1945. The marchers, most of whom were out of work during the depression, wanted the money then. President Herbert Hoover ordered the Army to drive the veterans out of the shanty village they had built. A detachment of cavalry under Army Chief of Staff Douglas MacArthur routed the veterans from their quarters.

In 1968, Chicago—once again a center of dissent and violence—was a scene of what later investigators called a "police riot." During the Democratic National Convention, a protest group called the Yippies called a mass meeting in Lincoln Park. Police ordered it broken up by 11 p.m. When the demonstrators, mostly young people, refused to leave, police fired tear gas into them and charged in swinging clubs.

Many other recent examples of violent reaction to essentially peaceful dissent could be given. Policemen have often over-reacted to the provocations of demonstrators. Faced by an angry, advancing body of students at Kent State University in Ohio in May, 1970, National Guardsmen opened fire, killing four students. A week later in Jackson State College in Mississippi, police fired more than 150 rounds of ammunition into a crowd of students outside a girls' dormitory. Two were killed and twelve injured. In both instances there were provocations. Students at Kent had previously burned a campus building. At the time of the shooting they were certainly confronting the guardsmen. At Jackson, rocks and bottles had been thrown at police. In both instances, there were unsubstantiated rumors of sniper fire against police. Still, police and guardsmen in both places have been accused of over-reaction, using bullets against rocks and cat-calls.

62

It is a distortion, however, to offer only examples of violent repression of dissent. At many times strikes have occurred without police interference. Officers have protected Negroes and prevented lynchings. Civil rights demonstrations have been unmarred by violence because policemen were present.

In modern times, the record of the police in *protecting* dissenters is even more marked. For over twenty years, strikes by workers have met virtually no resistance from police. Policemen maintain order and prohibit violence by either management or labor. The strike is allowed to run its course until settled by the company and the workers.

"Formal" lynchings are a thing of the past, more because of police protection than public attitudes. No longer do mobs of whites find a Negro and "string him up." The murders of black people are simply that—murders: clandestine shootings and bombings.

In the sit-in era of the civil rights movement there were thousands of instances in which demonstrations occurred without violence. In fact, many of the protests became a ritual. Arrangements were made in advance between the demonstrators and police. An agreed-upon number of protesters would show up at a particular location at a predetermined hour. The demonstrators would carry out certain actions, attempting to enter segregated facilities, singing songs, praying, marching in a certain area. Police would allow this to go on for a given period of time, then arrest a pre-decided number of demonstrators. Some would be led to the waiting vans. A certain number would be carried. In short, in many instances, police and demonstrators learned to cooperate to avoid bloodshed, while permitting the dissent to achieve its purpose.

The most recent examples of relations between dissenters and police should not be limited to the violence at Kent, Jackson, and Chicago. Early in 1970 an estimated one million people marched on Moratorium Day in behalf of peace. The demonstrations occurred in a number of cities, yet there was very little violence.

What can be made of all this? When does violent repression occur?

Obviously, the record is spotty. The United States has a long history both of violent repression of peaceful dissent and of allowing such dissent to occur unmolested. Is there any pattern governing the occurrence of violent repression? Certainly not with regard to the lynchings and murders of black people, which have been mere hooliganism and racism protected by the police and courts, a breakdown of the legal and law enforcement processes of America.

But there is a pattern to the violence of the labor disputes, sit-ins, and campus altercations. In most instances, the police and soldiers involved were acting in behalf of what is customarily called "law and order."

The strikers were violating laws against strikes, interfering with rights of property, disobeying court orders to end the strike, or obstructing the then-lawful privilege of management to fire strikers and hire scabs. The civil rights demonstrators were violating segregation laws and trespass regulations, interfering with property rights.

64

Campus protesters were breaking laws against disorderly conduct, seizing property owned by universities, resisting arrest, provoking disturbances by inflammatory speeches and actions. They were flouting lawful authority. Large gatherings of angry, dissatisfied, threatening people, assembled for whatever purpose, are hardly a contribution to public tranquility.

Though people speak of "law and order" the two don't necessarily go together. When laws are improper and unjust, they contribute to *disorder*, not order. The strikers felt their wages, hours, and working conditions were unjust, as were the efforts to break their strike. The civil rights demonstrators believed the segregation laws and the laws restricting voting rights were illegal. The campus demonstrators believed that the War in Vietnam was both illegal and immoral and that the educational and admission policies of the university were incorrect and unfair. In all instances, the dissenters tried to use their constitutional rights of assembly and free speech to dramatize and call attention to their situation and beliefs, to have the laws and policies changed, and to correct what they considered injustice. Thus an almost inevitable clash developed between constitutional rights of dissent and the law as enforced by police. The result was not order but disorder.

Even a cursory study of American history shows that, thus far, constitutional rights have prevailed over laws. In a democracy, no matter how imperfect it may be, laws reflect the will of the majority and those laws are subject to change when conditions and attitudes change. Thus far, the constitutional guarantees of assembly and free speech have remained unabridged except for brief periods.

When police have sought to repress dissent, they have played into the hands of the dissenters, particularly the more militant or radical leaders. Violence by police has led to violence by strikers. Militant anarchists or communists who recommended violence were able to enlist moderates to their beliefs because of the anger and dismay which police violence produced. Police repression of nonviolent civil rights demonstrations did more to enlist public opinion against segregation and voting restrictions than all the speeches of Dr. King. On many campuses, police brutality "radicalized" moderate students, creating more dissent and frequent violence.

Teenager David Romano, a student in Westport, Connecticut, presented a description of this phenomenon in *The High School Revolutionaries*. He was present when police charged into the Yippies at Lincoln Park in Chicago in 1968. He wrote:

For the first time in my life I actually encountered oppression of an outright fascist nature, where the right of the people to free assembly and to make their views known was being intentionally thwarted. It was being thwarted by the power structure no matter what the costs in life and limb to those people out on the street. If they could not be made to go indoors peaceably, then they were going to be clouted over the head with a club, dragged away, and put in a cell. It was this experience that first got me started in radicalism.

66

It has been a standard technique of radical dissent for at least a century to provoke police into violence so that the David Romanos, in their shock and dismay, will be converted to dissent. When police have been more impartial, seeking to uphold the rights of assembly and peaceful dissent, rather than laws enforcing the status quo and order, there has been considerably less violence and radicalization.

Among the outspoken advocates of this position was the late General George M. Gelston of the Maryland National Guard. He gained experience in civil disorders when he commanded troops occupying Cambridge, Maryland, during civil rights disturbances. Later, he was interim chief of Baltimore Police during demonstrations there.

During an interview he emphatically denied the effectiveness of court injunctions, arrests, and other police interference with assembly, free speech, and dissent. He maintained that all Americans have a constitutional right to such actions and that the role of police is solely to protect them in those rights. During civil rights demonstrations seeking to integrate apartment houses in Baltimore, he had his "cops" out in force. But they took no action other than to separate and protect the demonstrators and a large hostile crowd of onlookers led by members of the Ku Klux Klan in full regalia. He ordered all vehicular traffic out of the area.

At one point demonstrators sought to provoke police by sitting in the street, blocking it. A police inspector suggested they should be arrested for blocking traffic. Gelston replied, "I don't see any traffic." No arrests were made and, after a while, the street sitters got up and left.

Another time, apartment house owners obtained a court order limiting the number of pickets in front of a building to ten, who were to be quiet and orderly. More than fifty singing and chanting pickets showed up. Gelston quickly lost his ability to count or hear, and refused to make arrests. This led one of the pickets to remark, "I'm willing to be arrested. I'm willing to go to jail. But I am not willing to stand out here and march all day."

Gelston maintained he was merely keeping policemen neutral. He permitted dissent about apartment house segregation and refused to allow the issue to be diverted by interjecting the question of police brutality. More and more police officials around the country are adopting such practices, though incidents of police violence still continue.

Because police, sometimes reinforced by troops, have thus far overwhelmed violent dissent, there is a temptation to assume that violent repression will also overwhelm peaceful dissent. History does not necessarily indicate this. Reaction against the repression of strikers led to laws insuring the rights of labor unions to strike and protecting them from strikebreaking methods of management. Reaction against the repression of civil rights protesters led to repeal of segregation laws and legislation protecting voting rights. Reaction against the repression of peace protesters contributed to growing unpopularity of the War in Vietnam, a change in the conduct of the war starting under President Johnson and continuing under President Nixon who has expressed a desire to end American involvement in Southeast Asia as soon as possible.

Thus, as so often in the past, the following situation seems to exist today: Knowing that repression will only increase dissent, radical dissenters seek to provoke police violence by taunts, unruly conduct, bottle throwing, and similar acts. For police to respond to confrontation and to use repressive measures can give the victory to the dissenters. A wiser course for police seems to be to allow the demonstration to take place, remain neutral, avoid a confrontation, and repress only the violent actions of demonstrators.

Admittedly, there is often a fine line between provocation and violent demonstration, but policemen have had to make this distinction for a long time. Greater efforts at neutrality and more cooperation with the demonstrators should help police cope with a difficult problem. The law may often provoke disorder, but it is possible for police, using restraint, to maintain order.

Chapter 4
Separatism
and Boycotts

A COMMON, though frequently curious form of dissent throughout American history has been physical separation. The Pilgrims were separatists from the established Church of England. They traveled to the New World to establish a community where they could worship as they pleased.

In one form or another, Americans have been expressing this type of dissent ever since. Today there are several examples of it. One relatively small example, which has nevertheless received huge publicity in the press and on television, is the "hippie commune." A band of people, many of them young, take over a farm or other acreage and establish a communal type of life. The practices of these communes are reported to include a back-to-nature movement, emphasis on free thought and uninhibited actions, absence of restriction, some use of drugs and

71

narcotics, and considerable sexual license. By living in this manner, the members of a hippie commune are expressing their dissent from a society which, in their opinion, emphasizes the opposite of all these practices.

Another current example is black separatism. Many militant Negroes shun integration in America and advocate separation of the races, for they consider integration with whites impossible. They would turn the black ghettos of cities into communities governed and controlled economically by Negroes. The Black Muslims have already made progress in carrying out such ideas. Proclaiming loyalty to the Moslem religion, the Black Muslims have established farms, factories, and other business enterprises owned and operated by members of the sect.

Do these illustrations have any parallels in the past? Does the long history of separatism and communal living in America offer any clues to what might happen in the modern era?

There are plenty of parallels, for going off somewhere to establish a utopian community is as American as popsicles. Hundreds of communities have been established, most of them by religious sects who considered the world so sinful that the only recourse was to withdraw from it and establish communities of true believers practicing the true religion and true life style. Among the most famous of these was the "United Society of Believers in Christ's Second Coming," more commonly known as the Shakers, from the trembling that occurred among them during moments of religious emotion.

Between 1780 and 1874, the Shakers established fifty-eight communities wherein they practiced celibacy, confession, and common ownership of property, pacifism, equality of the sexes, and consecrated work. Many of the communities lasted a long time, although celibacy made it difficult to sustain the population. By 1960 the Shakers were virtually extinct.

The Shakers, along with many other religious communities, sought, in the words of Arthur Eugene Bestor, Jr., in his book *Backwoods Utopias*, "to withdraw from all contact with the state, with force and secular power, and in a voluntary union to realize the evangelical law of God." He said they tried to build a "society within a society."

Vestiges of these ideas exist in the Amish and Mennonite communities in Ohio and Pennsylvania. Members of these religious sects seek to separate themselves from the mainstream of America by tenaciously holding on to old styles of dress and transportation, customs, methods of farming, and attitudes about education and politics. By the standards of most Americans, the Amish are anachronisms, yet they stubbornly maintain the virtues of the past and lead useful and productive lives.

Religious differences have not been the only reason for separatism. Political and economic ideas have spawned many a community. Among the most famous was Robert Owens' New Harmony, founded in 1825.

Owens was an Englishman who rose from poverty to become a wealthy textile manufacturer. But with a difference. He had a social conscience in days of child labor and wage slavery. At New Lanark, England, he

73

established a model factory town. He abolished child labor in his factories, established free public schools, raised wages, shortened working hours, sold goods in the company store at cost, and substituted advice for punishment. There were no police or courts. When a business slump temporarily closed his mill, Owens paid his workers full wages. His "utopia" at New Lanark was the talk of Europe.

Owens wanted to do more. He felt that individualism was an evil. "Until the individual system shall be entirely abandoned, it will be useless to expect any substantial, permanent improvement in the condition of the human race." He wanted to establish cooperative societies where people worked and lived together and shared all in common. He came to America to carry out his scheme.

He was heartily welcomed. On two occasions he addressed the House of Representatives. Two Presidents, James Monroe and John Quincy Adams, talked with him. Most of the intellectuals of the time were swept up by his ideas. "The rich and the poor, the governors and the governed have but one interest—common happiness."

To establish his utopia Owens paid $150,000 for the town of Harmony, Indiana. It was a religious community of 30,000 acres established by 600 Germans in 1814. The Germans, led by George Rapp, moved to a new town, Economy, Pennsylvania, leaving New Harmony to the Owenites.

Owens made serious mistakes. He made no effort to screen the applicants or to figure how much money it would cost to operate the community. Anyone was allowed to settle in New Harmony and dissension quickly developed. Recurrent financial problems forced Owens to permit the establishment of capitalistic businesses. These grew and prospered, while the cooperative, communistic society withered away. Owens returned to England where he was active in the trade union movement.

Almost twenty years later came the "Phalanx." Philosopher of this utopian scheme was Charles Fourier, a Frenchman. He envisioned a community, called a phalanx, consisting of 400 to 2,000 men and women who would live together in a common building. The members would be organized into various groups, each of which would be assigned a task, such as planting crops, harvesting them, making shoes, or whatever. Each member would be free to join the group he wished or to move among the groups to avoid boredom. Fourier foresaw greater productivity and happier workers.

The Frenchman was no socialist or communist. He saw capitalists and laborers existing side by side. Everyone would have his necessities provided for. The substance left (or profits) would be divided as follows: four twelfths to capital, five twelfths to labor, and three twelfths to talent. Labor was further divided into necessary, useful, and agreeable. Those who performed necessary work received the greatest rewards.

Fourier's ideas were brought to America by Albert Brisbane, a wealthy young American idealist. He wrote and made speeches and soon attracted a following of intellectuals. Fourier study groups were established nationwide. Thirty-four phalanxes were set up, attracting about 8,000 people, but all were undermanned and underfinanced. None lasted more than a few years. The most famous was Brook Farm, to which such writers as Emerson, Hawthorne, and Thoreau belonged.

One more utopian community must be mentioned, Oneida in New York. Established in 1848 by the Perfectionists led by John Humphrey Noyes, Oneida lasted until 1881. Two features of Oneida stand out. First, it was financially successful, prospering both in farming and in manufacture. It never did fold, but was reorganized into a stock company. Second, its communistic ideas extended also to sex. Every woman was considered the property of every man there, but male continence (not female continence) was to be practiced. Propagation of children was permitted only to "scientifically" paired couples who were calculated to produce the best offspring.

Since the first settlers came to this country, the frontier has offered dissent through separation. To a limited extent this is true today.

There were many reasons why settlers came to the New World and then gradually pushed westward until the whole land was populated. Settlers were motivated by hopes for wealth, adventure, need to escape punishment, longing for open spaces and a new start in life. But at least some of the successive generations of frontiersmen were motivated by dissent. Packing up their families and possessions, Americans moved to the frontier to express their dissatisfaction and disapproval with the quality of life they had known before. Some were dissenting from particular political, social, or economic situations. The vastness of America permitted this sort of individualistic dissent to go on for a long time.

With a population of over 200 million today, there are very few areas in the continental United States where a man can find a frontier. Only Alaska still offers the opportunity. And there are Americans who find the lure of this "last frontier" irresistible.

Many writers claim that something valuable was lost to the American character when the frontier disappeared. It certainly is more difficult today for a person to express in a physical way his individuality, independence, and spirit of adventure. Without the frontier as a means of expressing individual dissent, Americans are forced into greater conformity and involvement in a community. There are advantages to this, but it is a big adjustment for many people to make. Senator Eugene McCarthy, in commenting upon the murder of Senator Robert F. Kennedy in 1968, said Americans must realize that the frontier is gone and violent individual expressions of dissent cannot be tolerated.

Separatism has long appealed to the black man in America. Since colonial times, black Americans have sought to escape oppression by going somewhere else to live in freedom. Attempts were made to establish Negro communities in the West or in Central or South America, but the most consistent effort has been to return to Africa, the ancestral homeland of Negroes. There was some success. The African nation of Liberia was founded by American Negroes. Its leaders are descendants of Americans who returned to Africa.

77

Perhaps the most celebrated "back to Africa" movement was organized by Marcus Garvey in the 1920s. A West Indian by birth, Garvey came to America espousing the theme of black unity, urging the 400 million black people of the world to unite, demand their rights, and throw off the fetters of white rule. More than a million Americans were enlisted in his cause. He raised huge sums to transport Americans back to Africa. He organized factories and businesses and founded a steamship line. Ultimately, Garvey's schemes foundered on legal and financial difficulties, but his ideas of black unity bore rich fruit among the Black Muslims and others who advocate black solidarity and separatism today.

Relatively few black Americans suggest returning to Africa today. Even if it were physically and financially possible for 22 million Americans to return to Africa, the Africans do not want them, nor do the Americans much want to go. Black separatism today means living in a black community or ghetto, which runs its own political and economic affairs free from white control. The community would thus be free to practice its own customs, art, and traditions.

Those who advocate this goal—and a great many black people do not, insisting upon integration instead—are following a long-standing American tradition. The waves of immigrants to America first established ethnic communities. Germans, Irish, Poles, Italians, Jews, Chinese, and others separated themselves from other Americans, preserving their language, religion, and customs for generations. Each of these minorities came to exert political power; each came to wield economic power, owning homes, businesses, and factories.

The black man, so long legally and economically oppressed in America, is coming belatedly to the sense of community the Irish had a century ago. For 300 years after the first black slaves were imported in 1619, Negroes were dispersed over a large area. First as slaves, then as freedmen, they lived mostly in the South. They were predominantly rural and employed in agriculture. By the Civil War, for example, only 400,000 out of 4 million slaves lived in towns or cities of the south. There were Negro communities in Northern cities, but they were relatively small. Because black people were so widely dispersed, community action was extremely difficult. It was virtually impossible, for example, to organize collective dissent within the black community against lynching, segregated transportation and public accommodations, and voting restrictions.

Then, about 1917, the American Negro began one of the great migrations in history. For the next four decades, black people left the South as individuals and families, in an act of dissent against the conditions of life in the South. By that act, the majority of the Negro population of the United States was transformed from Southern rural to Northern urban.

With the gathering together of the Negro, community action became possible. Organizations were formed. Organized protests were held. The sit-ins and other protests of the Negro Revolution, which have already been described, were a product of community action. These toppled the legal basis of segregation, discrimination, and voting restrictions.

Today, the Negro vote is a potent political force. Economic power is growing. Negro arts are flourishing. Justified pride in being a Negro is visible everywhere. Most difficult problems remain in such areas as unemployment, poverty, education, health, crime, and white discrimination. An attack upon these problems can be made because black people, expressing dissent with their feet, are organized into a community where power and pride can be developed apart from white people.

Another form of dissent long used in America is the boycott. In its broadest sense, a boycott is an organized refusal by a group to use a product or service or to perform a service.

The Montgomery bus boycott was a classic example of dissent by boycott. By refusing to ride segregated buses in Montgomery, Negroes forced the bus line to abandon the policy and had laws requiring segregated seating declared unconstitutional.

Labor has long used the boycott. In fact it has been the principal weapon workmen have used in their struggle for better wages. A standard technique was to refuse to buy a product which did not display the "union label," that is, a mark affixed to the product signifying that it was made by workers who belonged to a labor union. Boycotts of non-unionmade products were a primary method by which labor organizations grew in numbers and power.

A recent example of a boycott involved California table grapes. Workers led by Cesar Chavez organized a boycott which went on for five years. It attracted the support of many prominent people and spread nationwide, even to other countries. Both the sales and price of California grapes went down. Finally, in August, 1970, leading California growers settled with Chavez' union for higher wages and agreed to affix the union label to boxes of grapes.

In a sense the strike is a boycott, with workers refusing to perform a service until demands for wages or other benefits are met or a compromise reached. It is a potent method, for it makes it virtually impossible for a manufacturing company to operate. If the company is a store or restaurant, or performs a service, the picket line set up by workers usually keeps customers away. Quite recently the strike has been used by students to protest educational policies or even the war in Indochina. By boycotting classes, students make their dissent highly visible.

To be effective the boycott or strike must be highly organized. If it is a strike, close to 100 percent of the men must refuse to work. Production must be halted. If this does not occur, the strike has no chance of success. In the boycott, all or nearly all buyers or users must participate. And the boycott must go on for a long time. The Montgomery bus boycott continued for over a year, the grape boycott for five. Organization and discipline must be of a high order.

Also, to be effective, the grievance leading to the boycott or strike must be genuine. Strikes frequently failed when public opinion turned against the strikers. The grape boycott was effective because a large number of people supported the workers and refused to buy grapes.

Finally, the effective strike or boycott is non-violent.

81

Violent acts by strikers or boycotters bring police repression and turn off public support. Students, for example, who both strike and riot on a college campus are diluting one of the most effective forms of dissent with one of the least effective.

Chapter 5
The Printed Word
and Television

FROM COLONIAL TIMES until the present, the printing press has offered a method of expressing dissent. Through newspapers, magazines, pamphlets, posters, books, cartoons, and pictures, the dissenter has attacked the "establishment" and sought to rally supporters to his viewpoint.

Today's "underground press" and spate of books urging revolution are the latest in a long line of dissenting publications that includes the Declaration of Independence, Thomas Paine's *Common Sense*, William Lloyd Garrison's *Liberator*, the *Crisis* published by the NAACP, the *Daily Worker* of the Communist Party, and Rachel Carson's *The Silent Spring*. There have been over the years hundreds of thousands of publications expressing dissent. Indeed, the nature of the publishing business is such that it perhaps prints more dissenting than majority viewpoints, if only because controversy sells.

The printed word has always offered one of the most effective means of dissent. This can be illustrated by two publications, written a century apart.

For more than thirty years, William Lloyd Garrison was one of the nation's foremost advocates of the abolition of slavery. Born in Massachusetts in 1805, Garrison was a mild-mannered man, but he was capable of vitriolic prose. First through a Baltimore newspaper and then through the *Liberator*, which he began publishing on January 1, 1831 in Boston, Garrison attacked slavery and all who advocated or assisted it. In his opening editorial he wrote:

I *will be* as harsh as truth and as uncompromising as justice. On this subject I do not wish to think, or speak, or write with moderation . . . I am in earnest—I will not equivocate—I will not excuse—I will not retract a single inch—AND I WILL BE HEARD.

Garrison carried on his crusade until the Civil War. He was against gradualism. He wanted all slaves freed instantly.

Has not the experience of two centuries shown that gradualism in theory is perpetuity in practice? Is there an instance in the history of the world where slaves have been educated for freedom by their taskmasters?

He was against paying slaveowners for their property,

likening it to paying a thief for giving up stolen property. He flailed any and all public figures who aided or abetted slavery, including Daniel Webster and Henry Clay, who compromised the slavery issue to save the Union.

Garrison was assailed and assaulted. Virginia authorities charged that Nat Turner had read the *Liberator* to his followers before launching his insurrection. Rewards as large as $5,000 were offered to anyone who could arrest and bring Garrison to trial. In 1835, an angry mob dragged Garrison through the streets of Boston. Only the intervention of police, who jailed him, saved his life. In New York, he was jeered by thousands of people. Several of his supporters were attacked. In Illinois, Elijah P. Lovejoy, who published a newspaper similar to Garrison's, was murdered and his press destroyed.

Perhaps more than any other man, Garrison inflamed abolitionist sentiment in the United States. Most of the influential intellectuals of the North were won to the cause. Indeed, the Republican Party sprang from the soil of abolition in the Midwest.

Yet, the astounding fact is that the *Liberator*, Garrison's voice in all this, never had a circulation any larger than 3,000!

A century later Americans considered chemical pesticides, such as DDT, to be an unmitigated blessing, evidence of man's progress against the elements. In a single small volume, *The Silent Spring*, laden with facts and rather scholarly in tone, Miss Rachel Carson drastically altered the nation's thinking. Hundreds of thousands of Americans read Miss Carson's poignant revelations of the dangers chemical pesticides posed to birds, animals, plants, and other forms of wildlife. The search for non-chemical methods of pest control, indeed, the nation's entire interest in ecology and pollution control, began with Rachel Carson.

These are but two of the many examples of the power of the printed word. How was it possible for William Lloyd Garrison, publishing a magazine with a circulation of less than 3,000, and Rachel Carson, citing the dangers of what everyone thought was a great blessing, to have such an immense effect on public opinion?

The power of the printed word stems from the fact that only a small percentage of the population are leaders in any field of endeavor. But these few men and women are tremendously important and powerful because they carry along many millions of people with them.

One of the major reasons for the influence of these people is that they read material that is informative and thought-provoking. They absorb the facts and ideas of others and develop their own thinking in a particular area. Consider the late Malcolm X. He had very little formal schooling. Imprisoned for a crime, he taught himself to write expressively by laboriously copying the dictionary. He went on to read widely in history, political science, and philosophy. From this he developed his ideas of black solidarity which came to influence the thinking of large numbers of black people.

The 3,000 who read the *Liberator* were very influential. They learned about Garrison's views, told others about them, incorporated them into their own writings, and thus carried Garrison's message to a far wider circle than his publication reached. Millions of people who had never read a word that Garrison ever wrote learned about him and either praised or denounced him. In an era of mass education, Miss Carson influenced vast numbers of people in a similar manner.

The writers and editors of today's dissenting "underground" press face some difficulties, however, which their counterparts in the past did not. Publishing is a major industry today. More than a hundred thousand books are published annually in the United States. There are numerous newspapers, magazines, trade journals, scholarly publications, quarterlies, pamphlets, and other printed materials vying for the attention of a rather small audience.

The biggest problem with the underground press is television, the famous (or infamous) "wasteland" or "boob tube." Prior to 1950, most Americans learned their news from newspaper accounts (and radio broadcasts in the 1930s and 1940s). Except for the few hundred people present at the Haymarket Riot, all anyone knew of the facts was what the newspapers told them. And it must be remembered that until about 1920 most newspapers made little pretense of impartiality. News was reported in an outrageously distorted manner to influence the paper's readers. The only saving grace was the number of newspapers in those days, each with a distinct bias. Most people tended to read the paper they agreed with. To a certain extent this is true of the underground press today.

87

Americans are no longer dependent upon the printed word for news. They see it on television. But do they? To give only one of thousands of examples: In 1968, network television showed rioting during the Democratic National Convention in Chicago. The TV picture showed demonstrators and police scuffling, but Americans saw neither the beginning nor the end of the riot, nor the provocations, the causes, or the reasons for the actions that appeared on the screen. Americans saw not news, but an *episode* of the news. They were sharply divided in their reactions to what they saw, some favoring the police, others the demonstrators. How many of those millions of viewers realized they were seeing only *part* of the news?

The television camera has had an immense effect on dissent in America. A battle between police and protesters is no longer a distant event occurring thousands of miles away and read about next day. The battle is happening right then in millions of living rooms, leaving viewers to form their own impressions or reactions to what they witnessed. Because television reaches so many millions of people and has such an impact upon them, often dissenters have abandoned the printed word in favor of television. But buying time on television is prohibitively expensive. Therefore, dissenters have developed techniques for "getting on" television news.

The technique is dictated first by the realization that the television camera is an expensive and bulky instrument. A television station has only a limited number of cameras. For a live broadcast, the camera has to be transported in a truck which provides power for the camera, lights, and other paraphernalia. Even if the action is to be filmed for later showing, there is a logistics problem. A camera must be loaded with film, a man must run it and, usually, another man must operate equipment to reproduce the sounds.

The journalist needs only a pencil and paper, or at most a small tape recorder. He can arrive after an event and learn what happened by questioning observers. But the television camera must be working at the time the event occurs. Therefore, if you wish to get on television, you must do something that will interest millions of people and you must either do it where cameras are set up or give the television cameramen enough time to arrive and set up their equipment.

What sort of an event is likely to make television news? Directors of television news programs are public spirited and responsible. News programs endeavor to report briefly the most important news and comment of the day with as much fairness and balance as possible. But TV news cannot consist solely of an announcer, no matter how attractive, sitting there reading the news for fifteen minutes. TV news must have film which *illustrates* the news and the content of the news program is, therefore, frequently determined by the illustrative film that is available.

Nor can that illustrative film consist solely of the President or some other public figure making a statement. The chief purpose of the movie camera and the chief interest of those who view its product is the reproduction of *action*. Television news must have action film, a movie of people doing something.

Dissenters can manage this without much difficulty.

Dressing bizarrely, marching up and down, and shouting provide ample action. Even better is a scuffle with police, a full-blown riot, a burning building, or a few bullet-riddled bodies lying around. This is *not* to say that all television violence is staged; however, efforts to provide action for the television cameras do often lead to violence. Considering the logistical problem of the cameraman and the amount of disorder and violence shown on television news, we may conclude that there is probably strategy as well as spontaneity involved.

Television, then, has the effect of emphasizing and encouraging the more visual forms of dissent at the expense of the more thoughtful and orderly varieties. If it does not encourage violence, it at least makes it more likely to occur. Also, the emphasis upon visual dissent distorts reality. There is no more—probably less—violent dissent in America today than in various periods of the past. The electronic eye of the camera, however, by depicting so much of the violence that does occur, suggests the contrary.

Chapter 6
The Ballot Box

To MOST Americans the ballot box is the best expression of dissent. The majority of Americans believe that if a person doesn't like what is going on, he should go to the polls and vote for people who will do as he wishes.

The American form of government reflects this belief. Members of both houses of Congress are elected by voters to represent them in enacting laws and solving problems. The President is also elected by the people to administer laws and provide leadership in solving problems. State, city, and other local governments are modeled along the same pattern. It is an honored belief in America that if the elected representatives do not truly represent the people and solve their problems, they will be voted out of office in favor of more capable people.

In practice this theory breaks down—providing both advantages and disadvantages for dissenters.

To begin with, it is only on infrequent occasions that the voters of a district have a collective opinion to force upon their representatives. Perhaps the most common instances concern "bread and butter" issues. In an economic slump, the majority of voters recognize that "times are bad," with high unemployment, high prices, and a shortage of money. Voters have recognized and reacted *en masse* to such conditions, as well as to corruption in government, taxes and government spending, prohibition of alcoholic beverages and the elimination of that prohibition, law and order, extension of the vote to women, and the rights of blacks and other groups.

But there is no well-defined, easily-recognized voter sentiment on the majority of issues. Voters are less concerned about or not so familiar with such problems as balance of payments, regulation of airports, foreign policy, protective tariffs, customs rules, conservation, missile deployment, and a host of other issues.

Lacking a majority sentiment on such matters, voters expect the Congressman or Senator or President to be thoughtful and independent and to use his best judgment. Indeed, independence and leadership are frequently more highly prized by voters than slavish attention to pressure groups. A current example is Senator William Fulbright, chairman of the Senate Foreign Relations Committee. It is certainly open to doubt whether the majority of the voters of Arkansas agree with his views that the War in Indochina must be ended immediately. But there is no doubt that the majority of the voters of Arkansas admire his independence and courage.

Some members of the House of Representatives are elected by constituencies where the will of the people is known on particular issues. A representative from a predominantly Negro district would be expected to initiate and support programs promoting civil rights and social justice. A man from a factory district would be expected to favor labor legislation, and one from an agricultural area to support farm legislation. The representative of a "silk stocking" district would naturally come out for legislation favoring businessmen and investors.

These same representatives, however, would have no mandate on other issues. The Negro would have little instruction from his constituents with regard to the defense budget. The silk stocking congressman would probably not have to concern himself about voter sentiment on farm bills.

Thus, a congressman or senator or President is his own man on a majority of issues. Lacking pronounced voter sentiment, he acts as he thinks best. This fact affords a tremendous opportunity for dissenters. Great activity goes on continually in the United States to influence elected officials to support a particular viewpoint.

All this effort to influence the views of representatives is called "lobbying." It is a major industry in the United States. At the simplest level, the representative or the president is besieged with petitions, letters, telegrams, and phone calls in support of various views on particular issues. Delegations call upon him. His home or office may be picketed by protesters.

Some of this activity is spontaneous. Large numbers of

citizens write or telegraph officials in Washington daily to express their opinions and to urge compliance with them. Much of the lobbying is organized, however. A group or association of people will launch a campaign to influence Washington. A petition will be circulated. Thousands of letters, many of them identical, will be dispatched. Letters will be written to newspapers condemning or supporting the official in his actions.

The professional lobbyist, based in Washington, is paid by an industry or association to influence members of Congress or other officials. He sees that they receive information supporting his viewpoint. He "wines and dines" them. He tries to show an officeholder that other representatives share his views so that he does not stand alone. He encourages the representative to make political deals, that is, to throw his support behind one issue in return for support on an issue he favors.

The most important thing the professional lobbyist does is to spend money or raise money for the candidate. The lobbyist is able to make funds, frequently large amounts, available to representatives or candidates as campaign contributions in return for their support on a favored issue. In an era in which a candidate for United States Senator may spend a million dollars or more, such campaign contributions are of particular influence.

The problem for the dissenter seeking to influence congressmen is that a lot of people are trying to do the same thing. Senators and representatives are badgered daily with a barrage of attempts to influence them—much of it offering conflicting viewpoints. For example, conservationists and ecologists are presently lobbying for legislation banning the manufacture and use of DDT and other chemical pesticides as harmful to man and animals and upsetting to the balance of nature. At the same time, some farm groups and the chemical industry are lobbying for continued use of pesticides as helpful to agriculture and beneficial to a basic industry. A vocal segment of the population is lobbying for an immediate end to the war in Indochina. At the same time, other segments are urging a total war leading to victory, or some other solution that does not bear the stigma of an American defeat.

When a dissenter sets out to influence one representative to support his viewpoint, he is undertaking a rather large task. When he seeks to influence a majority of the members of the House and Senate to enact legislation, he is undertaking an immense one.

Failing to influence an elected official to adopt their views, dissenters may attempt to deny him reelection and to elect someone who endorses their views. By so doing the dissenters immerse themselves in what is variously termed the art, science, or disease of politics.

Politics in the United States is not a job for the amateur. A significant number of people work at it full time, having served long apprenticeships to learn its techniques. There are techniques for getting out the vote in behalf of a candidate and for discouraging voters who will not support him, for building up an image, for raising funds, for using advertising and other means of public exposure to greatest effect, for winning primaries, for gaining the support of business, labor, ethnic, and religious pressure groups, many of whom want opposite things. In a professionally managed campaign almost nothing is left to chance. The appearance of the candidate, his comments, the places he goes to campaign, the persons he seeks to appeal to are all carefully calculated. Indeed, they are so carefully calculated that they appear spontaneous and *un*calculated.

When the amateur enters politics, no matter how sincere and enthusiastic he may be, he risks making mistakes that defeat his purpose. In the spring of 1970, large numbers of peace advocates went to Washington to talk to members of Congress in hopes of influencing them to end the War in Indochina. They undoubtedly had considerable success, but there was also a lot of wasted effort. Delegations wasted time calling upon representatives who were already on the side of peace, and more time arguing with representatives who were firmly convinced that the war must be continued. A professional politician would have known in advance those senators and representatives who were undecided and concentrated his influence upon them.

In Brooklyn, student politicians worked hard in 1970 in the Democratic primary in behalf of the congressional candidacy of Peter Eikenberry, a peace candidate. They rang doorbells, made phone calls, circulated campaign literature and generally worked mightily to defeat Representative John Rooney, a long-time Democratic machine politician. Rooney won by a wide margin. In analyzing the reasons for their defeat, the students themselves de-

cided that they had been unfamiliar with the issues trou-
bling the Irish, Italian, Negro, and Jewish residents of the
district who had voted for Rooney, and to whom peace
was relatively unimportant. Also, students had ignored a
section which favored Eikenberry. A get-out-the-vote
campaign there might have been effective.

In New Jersey, Princeton University students worked
doggedly for peace candidate Lewis Kaden, yet he lost the
primary by a narrow margin to incumbent Representative
Edward Patten. The mistake there, students discovered,
was that in getting out the vote, they had got out supporters of Patten rather than supporters of Kaden.

These are characteristic mistakes of the amateur in
politics. The professional has his district carefully ana-
lyzed. He knows "where the ducks are," that is, those
who will vote for him or his candidate and those who can
be convinced to do so. He does not make the mistake of
getting out the vote for the opponent or ignoring his own
supporters. Nor is he so devoted to one issue that he
ignores the other issues that influence voters.

There is ample evidence that when the energies of
amateurs are properly directed by professional politicians,
their efforts can be of great importance. But when the
dissenter enters politics alone, he faces an uphill battle
against the professional politician.

Failing to influence incumbents or to elect candidates,
dissenters have a third choice under the American political
system. They can organize a political party.

Washington and John Adams were members of the
short-lived Federalist Party. Jefferson led the Democratic-

97

Republican Party which elected four presidents before 1828. The Whig Party elected two presidents prior to the Civil War when it disintegrated over the slavery issue. But these were not third parties. They were second parties which later disappeared. All other Presidents have been Democrats or Republicans. No third party has ever elected a president or even come close to it.

The Democratic Party was founded by Andrew Jackson. The Democratic National Convention, which first met to nominate President Jackson for a second term, is the oldest enduring political party in the United States. The Democrats have survived a split over slavery, blame for the Civil War, and long periods when they did not elect a President. From 1860 to 1932, only Grover Cleveland and Woodrow Wilson were Democrats.

The Republican Party was founded in 1856 principally over the slavery issue. It became the dominant party with the election of Abraham Lincoln in 1860 and remained so until the Great Depression of 1929. The economic disaster forged a Democratic majority which continued unbroken for thirty years until the election of General Dwight Eisenhower in 1952.

The most successful third party candidacy was that of Theodore Roosevelt in 1912. A former Republican President, he bolted his party and formed the Progressive or "Bull Moose" party. He received 29 percent of the vote. In 1925, Robert M. LaFollette of Wisconsin ran on a Progressive ticket and won almost 5 million votes, the most ever, but still only 14 percent of the vote. In 1968, George Wallace of Alabama did well to get 12 percent of

the vote.   In 1948, Henry A. Wallace ran as a Progressive
and J. Strom Thurmond as a Dixiecrat.   Each got about a
million votes or 2 percent of the total.   In 1912 and 1920,
Eugene V. Debs ran for President on the Socialist ticket,
getting almost a million votes each time.

Nor have third parties been very effective in electing
legislators at the federal, state, and local levels.   Only an
occasional mayor and a handful of congressmen or state
legislators have professed membership in a third party.

Thus, it would appear that the American political
system makes it extremely hard for dissenters to work
within the system.   Only with the greatest difficulty can
dissenters influence officials, elect sympathetic individuals,
or form a new political party.

Difficult, yes.   But the unvarnished fact is that throughout American history dissenters have overcome the difficulties and worked within the political system to effect
change.   Dissenters have used political methods to enact
anti-monopoly or "trust busting" legislation, protect labor
unions and their right to strike, institute prohibition and
repeal it, begin the graduated income tax, and much, much
more.

There is no better example of "using the system" to
change the system than the long struggle for women's
suffrage.   To convince men that women should be permitted to vote and hold office once seemed an impossible
task, yet women, led by such indefatigable fighters as
Susan B. Anthony and Elizabeth Cady Stanton, did just
that.   In the 1870s, Miss Anthony confronted voting
officials and demanded to be registered as a voter.   She

99

did, in fact, vote. Arrested for unlawful voting, she insisted upon being tried and upon going to jail in lieu of paying bond. The judge, not wishing to make a martyr of her, refused to send her to jail. At a later trial—itself a mockery of justice—she was convicted. Again, the judge would not send her to jail, even when she refused to pay the $100 fine he imposed.

Miss Anthony's experiences aroused women—and men —all over the country. The National-American Woman Suffrage Association was formed. It became a powerful lobby in state legislatures and in Congress. Women insisted upon the vote and received it with the passage of the Nineteenth Amendment to the Constitution in 1920.

Today, if anything, dissenters are using the political system to bring changes with greater effectiveness than in the past. The sit-in demonstrations and street protests that began the Negro Revolution in the mid-1950s compelled tremendous political change at the local, state, and federal levels. The black dissent also produced health, education, and poverty legislation which benefited Negroes.

More recently, protest and demonstrations have led to attempts to reform the Selective Service system by the appointment of a new director and the beginning of a lottery system for selecting men to be drafted.

Of even greater significance has been the political dissent of those protesting the war in Indochina. The protest began in the mid-1960s among a rather small group of people who believed that American military involvement in Vietnam was improper, immoral, and futile. The ranks of protesters swelled until millions of people were in dissent against continuation of the war. They influenced many senators and representatives to oppose the war, including many who had approved the war initially. The dissenters forced a halt to the bombing of North Vietnam in 1968. Many political pundits believe that this dissent forced President Johnson out of office, although he insists that he had already decided not to seek another term when the massive protests began. When Nixon ordered the invasion of Cambodia, thus extending the war, the resulting protests led Congress to limit funds for war in Cambodia and to seek to prevent further use of armed forces without congressional consent.

Perhaps the most astounding recent example of the effectiveness of dissent in influencing the political system occurred when Congress enacted and President Nixon signed a bill granting the vote to 18-year-olds. The Supreme Court has since ruled that 18-year-olds may vote in Federal elections, but not in state and local elections until the Constitution or individual state laws are amended. But whether entirely legal or not, the law passed by Congress is strong evidence of how dissent influences the political system. Clearly, Congress was seeking to involve the young high school and college dissenters in the political system by giving them the vote, a means of expressing dissent other than violence.

Most of these changes occurred because dissenters influenced officials and elected more sympathetic individuals. Much of the influence was brought to bear through petitions, letters, telegrams, and personal visits. But the most effective methods took place in the street. When millions of Americans take to the streets to protest government policy it is bound to influence politicians. It is a time tested method used by labor, women suffragettes, prohibitionists, and Negroes in the past.

The third party movement in the United States has also been successful in bringing about political change. Perhaps the best example is the Populist Party, founded in 1892. It was composed of farmers and workingmen who were united in protest against the wealth and corruption of big business. The Populists drafted a platform containing such statements as, "From the womb of governmental injustice we breed the two great classes of tramps and millionaires."

In 1892 the Populists nominated General James Weaver of Iowa. He polled a little over a million votes and carried four states with twenty-two electoral votes. Four years later, Populism dominated the Democratic Party. William Jennings Bryan made his famous "Cross of Gold" speech at the Democratic convention, saying, "You shall not press down upon the brow of labor this crown of thorns, you shall not crucify mankind upon a cross of gold." He was nominated by the Democrats—and by the Populists. Bryan, running on both tickets, lost to Republican William McKinley, but by a narrow margin.

What was the Populist program? They wanted free and unlimited coinage of silver; the right of farmers to exchange produce for United States Treasury notes; government ownership of railroads, telephone, and telegraph; a graduated income tax; the parcel post system; restrictions on immigration, an eight-hour day for wage earners;

popular election of United States Senators; the Australian ballot, an official ballot printed by the government and marked in secret, and the initiative and referendum wherein voters could originate or repeal laws.

Within twenty years all but the first three items in this program had been adopted—and there is today a new movement for public ownership of railroads. The Populist Party didn't last, but who could call it a failure?

In 1968, George C. Wallace, at the time a former governor of Alabama, ran as a third party candidate, appealing to conservative and anti-Negro voters. His was an act of dissent if there ever was one. He raised large sums of money. He and his supporters circulated petitions and gathered the signatures of more than 2 million voters, which enabled Wallace to be listed as a candidate in all fifty states, in itself a rare achievement for a third-party candidate. He campaigned all over the country, working himself to the point of physical exhaustion.

Wallace's dissent might be described as a dissent from dissenters. He sought to appeal to a wide variety of Americans who were either out-an-out racists or who were concerned about racial tensions and about the direction in which the nation was moving. His message was aimed at people who were alarmed at what they considered a breakdown in law and order as demonstrated by crime, riots, burnings, looting, clashes with police and soldiers, bombings, and talk of revolution. He appealed to individuals who feared the basic structure of America was changing because of a large Federal bureaucracy which was unresponsive to the demands and needs of the people, to conservatives who were opposed to the liberal programs which

103

had been proposed and enacted in the 1960s, and to the Southerners, Westerners, and Midwesterners who felt the nation was being run by an Eastern "establishment." Wallace offered little in the way of a positive program. His following was stuck together with the cement of negativism, but so was the Whig Party, which elected two Presidents, both of whom were succeeded by their Vice Presidents, in the pre-Civil War era.

Wallace did not win, although one of every eight voters across the nation supported him. He was not even successful in denying a majority to either Nixon or Humphrey, thus forcing the election into the House of Representatives. There, it was argued, Wallace would have been able to trade votes for powers in the new administration.

But was Wallace a failure? It is much too soon to determine the final results, but he achieved some preliminary success. President Nixon, who was most apt to be hurt politically by Wallace's candidacy, adopted a "Southern strategy." He chose Maryland Governor Spiro Agnew as his running mate, and sought to appeal to the border states of Maryland, Kentucky, and Tennessee, as well as Florida. In his campaign and in his first year in office, Nixon in general took a conservative position on most matters. It may be argued that he would have done so anyway, but the Wallace campaign must certainly have encouraged him. If nothing else, Wallace demonstrated that there was a large segment of the population which was conservative and dissatisfied.

Amidst all the violence and talk of revolution today,

there is considerable evidence that youthful dissenters plan to work within the political system much as their fathers and grandfathers did. A poll conducted in mid-1970 by Louis Harris illustrates this.

Attempting to measure student political intentions, Harris found that 65 percent of all college students believe working to elect better public officials is the most effective way to solve the nation's problems. Almost the same percentage rejected violence as the last resort to effect change. From interviews with a cross section of students from fifty colleges, Harris determined that 89 percent believe that public pressure can change government policies. He also discovered that 39 percent of the students personally planned to work in the 1970 election campaigns. Harris figured that if only one-tenth that number actually did work, there would be 200,000 of them. Harris said these workers "could well change American politics beyond recognition. The students could virtually swamp the political process."

Harris' statement smacks of exaggeration, but there is no doubt that large numbers of enthusiastic, dedicated political workers could seriously alter the professional conduct of politics. At the very least, the student involvement indicates that once again the American political system is accommodating dissent.

Chapter 7
Dissent Through
the Courts

ONE AFTERNOON in 1936, Lillian Gobitis, aged twelve, and her brother William, ten, came home from school in the small town of Minersville, Pennsylvania. The principal had said they were not to return to school until they agreed to salute the flag as their classmates did.

The Gobitis (pronounced Go-BITE-is) family belonged to the religious sect known as Jehovah's Witnesses. The Witnesses believe that their obligation to the law of God is superior to any laws enacted by governments. They also insist upon a literal interpretation of Exodus, Chapter 20, Verses 4 and 5, which reads:

> Thou shalt not make unto thee any graven image, or any likeness of anything that is in heaven above, or that is in the earth beneath, or that is in the water under the earth; thou shalt not bow down thyself to them nor serve them.

The Jehovah's Witnesses consider the American flag to be an "image" and therefore refuse to salute it.

When the Minersville Board of Education required that all pupils salute the flag and recite the Pledge of Allegiance, the Gobitis children refused and were sent home.

Failing to salute the flag was an act of dissent. And the dissent imposed a hardship on the Gobitis family. Under compulsory education laws, it meant that Lillian and William had to be sent to private schools. Their father, Walter Gobitis, couldn't afford that.

Mr. Gobitis tried to reason with school officials. He explained over and over that he and his family and other Witnesses meant no disrespect to the flag. They loved their country and were as patriotic as the next person, but their religious beliefs forbade worship of graven images.

The school board paid no attention and the Gobitis children were expelled. Walter Gobitis might have organized Witnesses to march in the streets in protest, or perhaps to sit down in front of school houses or burn the flag in protest. He might even have blown up school buildings and assassinated school officials as an expression of dissent.

Walter Gobitis did none of these. He went to court to have the school board requirement declared unconstitutional and illegal. Since Walter Gobitis was poor, the American Civil Liberties Union assisted him. ACLU lawyers argued that the school board requirement violated the First Amendment's guarantee of freedom of religion.

The Federal District Court upheld Gobitis, as did the Third Circuit Court of Appeals in Philadelphia. Then the case was taken to the United States Supreme Court.

It was argued in April, 1940. World War II had begun in Europe. The case attracted wide attention for it symbolized in the minds of many the battle between liberty and oppression. To others it symbolized a challenge to patriotism in a time of potential danger to the United States.

The high court decided 8-1 against the Gobitis family. The opinion was written by Justice Felix Frankfurter, a Jew, an Austrian by birth, and one of the great liberal jurists of the era. He called the case a "tragic issue" and a "clash of rights, not a clash of wrong." Yet, the flag, he said, is "the symbol of our national unity . . . the emblem of freedom in its truest, best sense. As such, the right of society to teach patriotism and national unity to a child takes precedence over the parent's religious teaching."

Dissenting in the case was Justice Harlan F. Stone, Frankfurter's long-time idol. Justice Stone said:

> It is a long step and one I am unable to take to the position that government may, as a supposed educational measure and as a means of disciplining the young, compel public affirmations which violate their religious conscience.

He said it was one thing to "elicit" expressions of loyalty and another to "command" them.

The Frankfurter opinion was roundly denounced in newspaper editorials and by law professors as "surrendering to popular hysteria." At the same time the opinion was praised by patriotic groups.

Walter Gobitis had lost—or had he? The dissent went

on. Another Jehovah's Witness case came to Court, this time involving the constitutionality of a city ordinance which required Witnesses to buy a license to sell their religious publications on street corners or door-to-door. By this time some personnel of the Court had been changed and the ordinance was upheld by only a 5-4 margin.

In dissent were Stone, now Chief Justice, and Justices Hugo Black, William O. Douglas and Frank Murphy. Not only did they disagree with the licensing case, but they also declared that they believed the Gobitis case to have been wrongly decided.

When another case involving flag salutes reached the Supreme Court in 1943, the Court reversed itself, 6-3.

The majority opinion by Justice Robert H. Jackson (who was one of the better writers ever to sit on the Court) was a ringing defense of both civil liberties and dissent.

A person gets from a symbol the meaning he puts into it, and what is one man's comfort and inspiration is another man's jest and scorn. . . .

Those who begin coercive elimination of dissent soon find themselves exterminating dissenters. Compulsory unification of opinion achieves only the unanimity of the graveyard. . . . It seems trite but necessary to say that the First Amendment was designed to avoid these ends by avoiding these beginnings. . . .

If there is any fixed star in our constitutional constellation, it is that no official, high or petty, can prescribe what shall be orthodox in politics, nationalism, religion or other matters of opinion or force citizens to confess by word or act their faith therein. If there are any circumstances which permit an exception, they do not now occur to us.

Now in dissent was Justice Frankfurter. He argued that it was up to the legislators and not the Court to decide such matters. But in so doing he penned these emotional words:

> One who belongs to the most vilified and persecuted minority in history is not likely to be insensible to the freedoms guaranteed by our Constitution. Were my purely personal attitude relevant, I should wholeheartedly associate myself with the general libertarian views in the Court's opinion, representing as they do the thought and action of a lifetime. But as judges we are neither Jew nor Gentile, neither Catholic nor agnostic. We owe equal attachment to the Constitution and are equally bound by our judicial obligations whether we derive our citizenship from the earliest or the latest immigrants to these shores.
>
> It (the Constitution) gave religious equality, not civil immunity. Law is concerned with external behavior and not with the inner life of a man. . . . One may have the right to practice one's religion and at the same time owe the duty of formal obedience to laws that run counter to one's belief.

The flag salute cases, as they are called, illustrate how a majority opinion can shrink in a very short time to become a minority opinion, thus placing the former majority in dissent.

The flag salute cases also illustrate one of the principal forms of dissent in America—action taken in the courts.

The court's defense of dissent has occurred in cases involving, among other issues, religious freedom, Negro rights, and the reapportionment of Congress and state legislatures.

There is a common theme to the stories of these cases. As in the flag salute cases, most of the dissenters were "little people" fighting an uphill battle in defense of an apparently hopeless cause.

Consider Steven I. Engle and four other parents of eleven children in the New Hyde Park School District on Long Island, New York. They objected to the recitation in school of a prayer officially sanctioned by the State of New York. They objected, even though there was no compulsion attached to the recitation of the rather general prayer.

Two parents were Jewish, one was Unitarian, one a member of the Ethical Culture Society, and one was a non-believer. They contended that the prayer conflicted with their religious beliefs. They objected to the stigma attached to their children when they did not participate in the prayers.

They went to court and lost at every level until they reached the Supreme Court. Then, in 1962, the Court, with a single dissent, declared school prayers a violation of the First Amendment. Justice Black wrote for the Court:

> It is neither sacrilegious nor anti-religious to say that . . . government in this country should stay out of the business of writing or sanctioning official prayers and leave that plainly religious function to the people themselves or to those the people choose to look to for religious guidance.

Shortly afterwards, the court declared all religious exercises in public schools unconstitutional.

The annals of the law in the United States contain no more dramatic and, at the same time, frustrating stories than the battle for equal rights for Negroes. For twenty years, the NAACP, under the leadership of Thurgood Marshall, now a member of the Supreme Court, fought to end school segregation in America.

School segregation, indeed the entire "separate but equal" doctrine which made second class citizens of black people, rested on an 1896 Supreme Court decision. To have that decision overruled seemed impossible, yet, starting in the 1930s, Marshall and his staff worked toward that goal. They brought case after case aimed at toppling the citadel of segregated education. They first attacked the separate but equal doctrine in university graduate schools. They won some cases and lost some, but ultimately major universities of the South were forced either to admit black students to white law schools or to establish entire schools for one student. Unable to do the latter, Southern law schools were integrated. Then, Marshall won a case in which segregated seating in university classrooms was declared illegal.

Beginning in 1950, Marshall launched an assault upon public school segregation. Five cases were filed from various sections of the country. The most celebrated was on behalf of Linda Brown, an eleven-year-old Negro child of Topeka, Kansas. She had been forced to attend segregated schools.

The case went to the Supreme Court and was argued and re-argued. The best legal minds in the country filed briefs on both sides. Then, on May 17, 1954, Chief Justice Warren, speaking for a unanimous Court, declared school segregation unconstitutional. He wrote:

> Does segregation of children in public schools solely on the basis of race, even though the physical and other tangible factors may be equal, deprive the child of the minority group of equal educational opportunities? We believe that it does.

Yet, this great victory turned hollow a few months later, when the Court ordered schools to be desegregated with "all deliberate speed." Most schools in the northern and border states were desegregated, but in the name of deliberate speed many Southern school districts set up legal roadblocks, one after another, to delay integration. Not until 1970, fifteen years later, did the Court order immediate integration of public schools.

If effective school integration lagged during those years, other forms of integration and discrimination were knocked down by the courts. The Supreme Court set the rule that there could be no state action to enforce segregation. In case after case, federal and state courts barred segregation in all publicly owned facilities and in privately owned accommodations which catered to the public.

One of the finest moments in the history of dissent in America began in the late 1950s when Charles W. Baker and other residents of Tennessee went to court in what had to be the "lostest" of lost causes. Baker contended he was a victim of unequal representation in the state legislature.

That certainly was true. Tennessee had last reapportioned its legislature in 1901 when the state had a population of 2,020,616 and 487,380 eligible voters. By 1960, Tennessee had a population of 3,567,087 and 2,092,891 eligible voters. In those nearly three score years, Tennessee had changed from a predominantly rural, farming area into a highly diversified state with four large cities—Memphis, Knoxville, Nashville, and Chattanooga—as well as many smaller cities. The residents of the metropolitan areas now worked in factories and stores, not on farms. Their problems, needs, and attitudes had changed.

But the legislature had not. Under the state's districting, Moore and Hamilton County each had the same number of representatives in the legislature, although Hamilton County had a population nineteen times larger than Moore County. The result was minority rule. 37 percent of Tennessee's voters elected twenty of the thirty-three state senators and 40 percent of the voters elected sixty-three of the ninety-nine members of the lower house.

The situation in Tennessee was merely typical. Similar, sometimes worse apportionment existed in nearly every state. Indeed, Congress itself was a study in unequal representation. One Michigan Congressman represented a district with 117,000 people, while another from the same state represented 802,000. Similar disparities existed in nearly every state.

And there was a pattern of discrimination to the unequal representation. The heavily populated districts were almost invariably urban and suburban. The people who lived in and near cities were underrepresented and discriminated against.

115

For decades urban voters had tried to change this situation. In Tennessee, representatives of cities and several governors had wanted to get the legislature to redistrict itself. But every attempt was rebuffed by rural legislators who appreciated the full extent of their political power, and as a result were unwilling to surrender even a fraction of it.

Likewise, many attempts had been made in the past to have the courts order redistricting, but these had always failed. The Supreme Court had stated that legislative apportionment, no matter how unfair it might be, was a political and not a judicial question. In the words of Justice Frankfurter, reapportionment was a "political thicket" which the Court should not enter.

Thus, when Charles Baker filed his suit in Tennessee, he was surely espousing a lost cause. Predictably, a three-judge Federal District Court panel dismissed Baker's action on the ground that the courts lacked jurisdiction. The issue went to the Supreme Court which heard arguments on the issue in 1960 and 1961. In fact, the justices heard three times as much oral argument as on a normal case.

To the delight of urban voters and the consternation of rural legislators, the Court said, in effect, that Baker had a point. By a majority of 6-3, the justices entered the political thicket. They said that apportionment was a matter for judicial action and sent Baker's case back to the District Court for trial. In a concurring opinion, Justice Tom Clark stated the Court's reasons for entering the thicket:

. . . I would not consider intervention by this Court into so delicate a field if there were any other relief available to the people of Tennessee. But the majority of the people of Tennessee have no practical opportunity for exerting their political weight at the polls to correct the existing "invidious discrimination." Tennessee has no initiative and referendum. I have searched diligently for other "practical opportunities" present under the law. I find none other than through the Federal Courts. . . . We . . . must conclude that the people of Tennessee are stymied and without judicial intervention will be saddled with the present discrimination in the affairs of their state government.

The rest is history. In a series of cases, the Supreme Court ordered both the United States House of Representatives and state legislatures, including both upper and lower houses, to reapportion themselves so that members came from districts of approximately equal population.

These rulings have been called the most important and far-reaching ever made by the Supreme Court. They returned the United States to a more representative form of government and enabled urban and suburban voters to begin to solve their problems by breaking the rural and parochial domination of Congress and state legislatures. One of the immediate effects was the passage in Congress in the late 1960s of a host of laws dealing with education, health, housing, poverty, and other urban problems.

Throughout history, but particularly in the 1950s and 1960s, the American court system has offered an effective way to express dissent. Time and again, the Court gave a hearing to the most obscure dissenter, with the most seem-

117

ingly farfetched cause—and very often sided with him. There is, however, another side to the judicial coin. The courts have been used consistently throughout history in attempts, sometimes successful, to suppress dissent.

Chapter 8
The Political Trial

A COMMON PRACTICE throughout American history has been to hail dissenters into court on some criminal charge stemming from their activity. But the criminal trial quickly turns into what is usually called a "political trial," with the main issues being the political, social, or other dissenting beliefs of the defendant. There have been thousands of such trials.

On December 30, 1905, Governor Frank Steunenberg of Idaho opened the gate of his home and was immediately blown to bits. Investigation showed that a fishing line with a bomb attached had been fixed to the gate. It was a clear case of murder and a reward of $15,000 was offered for the capture of the murderers.

James McParlan of the Pinkerton Detective Agency, the detective who had infiltrated and crushed the Molly Maguires 30 years before, was interested. Going to

Idaho, McParlan obtained a confession from one Harry Orchard, who said he had been hired for the murder by three men, William "Big Bill" Haywood, Charles Moyer, and George Pettibone. Haywood and Moyer were leaders of the Western Federation of Miners, a labor union which had staged a number of strikes in the area. Pettibone was a Denver businessman friendly to the miners' cause. To complete the skein of evidence against the three men, McParlan arrested Steve Adams, who, he said, corroborated Orchard's confession.

On February 12, 1906, warrants were issued in Idaho for the arrest of Haywood, Moyer, and Pettibone. But the three accused men were in Colorado. Arresting them there would involve prolonged hearings in Denver before they could be returned to Idaho, if indeed they could be returned. To get around this, the governor of Colorado secretly signed extradition papers on Saturday night, when the courts were closed. Haywood, Moyer, and Pettibone were arrested, placed on a train, and shipped to Idaho to face trial. McParlan told a Chicago *Tribune* reporter that the three men "will never leave Idaho alive."

Labor leaders and civil rights advocates were outraged all over the country. They called the arrest kidnapping and sought to have the men released on this ground. The kidnapping issue went to the Supreme Court, where the contention was denied. Eugene V. Debs, the Socialist labor leader, denounced the ruling in these words:

Kidnapping, then, being a legitimate practice, we all have a perfect right to engage in it. Let us take advantage of the opening. For every workingman kidnapped a capitalist must be seized and held for ransom.

As the trial approached, protests and demonstrations were held all over the country. Fifty thousand marched in Boston, 20,000 in New York. Moderate Samuel Gompers, head of the AFL, publicly castigated the authorities of Colorado and Idaho. The Socialist Party nominated Haywood for governor of Colorado while he was in prison.

The trial began on May 9, 1907. Leading the prosecution was Senator William E. Borah of Idaho, newly elected to office. For the defense was the famed Clarence Darrow, the foremost criminal lawyer of the time. He had been employed by the American Civil Liberties Union to defend the three men.

The state could offer only a weak case. Adams, the supposedly corroborating witness, repudiated his confession. This left the state with only Orchard's statements as evidence. Orchard, it developed, was an assumed name for a man who had a significant criminal record. Moreover, the defense produced a witness who testified he had heard Orchard threaten the dead governor.

But this was a political trial, not a criminal one. The actual crime of which the defendants were accused was secondary and Darrow knew it. In his summation to the jury, Darrow said the state was trying to kill the accused "not because it is Haywood, but because he represents a class." Darrow continued:

Don't be so foolish as to believe you can strangle the

Western Federation of Miners when you tie a rope around his neck. If at the behest of this mob you should kill Bill Haywood, he is mortal, he will die, but I want to say that a million men will grab up the banner of labor where at the open grave Haywood lays it down. . . . I speak for the poor, for the weak, for the weary, for that long line of men who, in darkness and despair, have borne the labors of the human race. Their eyes are upon you twelve men of Idaho tonight. If you kill Haywood your act will be applauded by many. . . . But if your verdict should be "not guilty" in this case, there are still those who will reverently bow their heads and thank these twelve men for the life and reputation you have saved.

The jury deliberated all night—and returned a verdict of not guilty for all three defendants. Orchard was given a life sentence.

World War I and the years immediately following it spawned a host of political trials in which hundreds of foreigners and radicals, particularly from the labor movement, were tried and jailed. Most of the arrests and trials came under the Espionage Act of 1917. That infamous law gave the government the right to censor newspapers, ban publications from the mails, and prosecute anyone who "interfered" with the draft or enlistment of soldiers. Conviction bore a punishment of up to twenty years in prison and a $10,000 fine.

Among the celebrated people imprisoned under the act was Eugene V. Debs. In 1919, he was old, tired, ill, but as a confirmed socialist and pacifist he deliberately set out to confront the Espionage Act. At Canton, Ohio, under the eyes of federal agents, he made a celebrated speech in which he paid tribute to the hundred who had been jailed.

The master class has always declared the war; the subject class has always fought the battles. The master class has had all to gain and nothing to lose, while the subject class has had nothing to gain and all to lose—especially their lives. . . .

Yes, in good time we are going to sweep into power in this nation and throughout the world. The sun of capitalism is setting; the sun of socialism is rising. . . . In due time the hour will strike and this great cause triumphant—the greatest in history—will proclaim the emancipation of the working class and the brotherhood of all mankind.

Debs was jailed. Released on bail, he made another speech against militarism. At his trial in 1918, Debs was at his most eloquent:

Your Honor, years ago I recognized my kinship with all living beings and I made up my mind that I was not one bit better than the meanest on earth. I said then, I say now, that while there is a lower class I am in it; while there is a criminal element, I am of it; while there is a soul in prison, I am not free. . . . Your Honor, I have stated in this court that I am opposed to the form of government; that I am opposed to the social system in which we live; that I believe in the change of both— but by perfectly peaceable and orderly means. . . . Let

123

the people take heart and hope everywhere, for the cross is bending, the midnight is passing, and joy cometh with the morning.

Debs was imprisoned in April, 1919. While in prison in 1920, he was nominated for President and received almost a million votes—an incredible accomplishment. Attorney General A. Mitchell Palmer, who had led the raids arresting Debs and other dissenters, urged President Woodrow Wilson to commute Debs' sentence, but the President refused. However, President Warren G. Harding freed Debs a few months later.

No political trial in American history was more celebrated than the one which began in Boston in 1920 with the arrest of two Italian immigrants, Nicola Sacco and Bartolomeo Vanzetti. Sacco was a shoe cutter by trade, Vanzetti a fish peddler. Both were anarchists active in the labor movement. On May 5, 1920, both were arrested and questioned about their radical activities. The following day they were charged with the murder of a paymaster and a guard during a payroll robbery near Boston. Vanzetti was also charged with another attempted holdup.

Vanzetti was tried on the latter charge first. In instructing the jury, Judge Webster Thayer said, "This man, although he may have not actually committed the crime attributed to him is nevertheless morally culpable, because he is the enemy of our existing institutions."

In June 1921, Sacco and Vanzetti were tried on the murder charge. Judge Thayer again presided. The criminal evidence in the case was at best inconclusive. The state produced witnesses who had seen Sacco and Vanzetti at the scene of the crime. The defense produced witnesses who located them many miles away. But, as in all political trials, the evidence of crime was of secondary importance. Judge Thayer told the jury the defendants were either "conscious of guilt as murderers or as slackers and radicals." In appealing for a conviction, he urged the jurors to remember "the American soldier boy . . . giving up his life on the battlefield of France," in World War I.

The jury found Sacco and Vanzetti guilty. The judge sentenced them to death. The case dragged through the appeals courts for six years. State legal officials submitted sworn affidavits that the two men were innocent and had been prosecuted solely for their political beliefs. Felix Frankfurter, the future Supreme Court Justice wrote:

> By systematic exploitation of the defendants' alien blood, their imperfect knowledge of English, their unpopular social views and their opposition to the war, the district attorney invoked against them a riot of political passion and patriotic sentiment; and the trial judge connived at —one had almost written cooperated in—the process.

The Sacco-Vanzetti case became a *cause célèbre* around the world. Strikes and demonstrations were staged in a score of world capitals. Isadora Duncan, the celebrated dancer, threatened to dance naked in front of the American Embassy in Paris to protest the conviction. When the men were executed in August 1927, a quarter of a million people marched in silence through the streets of Boston. In Paris 150,000 protesters rioted.

Vanzetti had the last word. His final letter written from prison in halting English contained these words:

> If it had not been for these things, I might have live out my life talking at street corners to scorning men. I might have die, unmarked, unknown, a failure. This is our career and our triumph. Never in our full life could we hope to do such work for tolerance, for joostice, for mans' onderstanding of man as now we do by accident. Our words—our lives—our pains—nothing! The taking of our lives—the lives of a good shoemaker and a poor fish peddler—all! That last moment belongs to us— that agony is our triumph.

The year 1925 saw a celebrated political trial of a different sort. Tennessee passed a law forbidding the teaching of Darwin's theory of evolution in public schools. Only the version of the Creation as told in the Bible could be taught. John T. Scopes, a young biology teacher in Dayton, Tennessee, began a test of the law with the aid of the American Civil Liberties Union. Arrested, Scopes became a figure in one of the celebrated trials of all time, the "Monkey Trial," so named because Darwin's theory claimed that man descended from early, now extinct apes.

For the prosecution was the master orator, William Jennings Bryan. Clarence Darrow appeared once again for the defense. Bryan defended the Bible and fundamentalist religion. Darrow defended academic freedom and the principle of separation of church and state. Scopes was convicted, but later freed on a technicality. Forty years later, Tennessee repealed its law.

After World War II another wave of anti-Communist hysteria led to a number of political trials. Communists, suspected Communists, individuals who had been Communists in the past, or simply persons who refused to say what they had been were tried on a variety of charges ranging from treason to contempt of Congress. The reputations of a number of prominent people were besmirched for little more than the suspicion that they had known or associated with a Communist in the past.

One political trial was particularly famous. In August 1948, magazine editor Whittaker Chambers admitted that in the past he had been a Communist courier transmitting confidential government documents to the Russians. He stated that Alger Hiss had helped him in this work.

Alger Hiss was a former law secretary to Justice Oliver Wendell Holmes, and a government official. He had risen to high rank in the State Department, serving as adviser to various international conferences and as a coordinator of foreign policy. Shortly before Chambers made his charges, Hiss had resigned from the State Department to become president of the Carnegie Endowment for International Peace.

The accusations against Hiss were exactly what many Americans wanted to hear, for at that time Senator Joseph R. McCarthy was making exaggerated charges that the State Department was "riddled" with Communists and spies. The accusation against Hiss seemed to corroborate these accusations.

Hiss denied the charges. Since the statute of limitations had expired, Hiss could not be charged with espionage. He was tried on a charge of perjury, that is, that he had lied about his Communist associations.

Hiss was tried twice, in 1949 and 1950. The first trial resulted in a "hung jury," that is, the jury could not agree on a verdict. At the second trial, Hiss was convicted and sentenced to five years in prison. Released in 1954, he wrote a book in which he again denied the allegations against him.

The trials of Alger Hiss sharply divided the country, generally along the lines of liberals and conservatives. President Truman called the issue a "red herring" and Secretary of State Dean Acheson defended his former associate. Even after Hiss was convicted, many liberals refused to believe he was guilty. Conservatives, however, felt the conviction was justified.

The most celebrated of recent political trials involved the "Chicago Seven"—David Dellinger, Rennie Davis, Tom Hayden, Abbie Hoffman, Jerry Rubin, John Froines, and Lee Weiner. They were tried for conspiring to incite a riot during the 1968 Democratic National Convention in Chicago and on the lesser charge of individually crossing state lines with intent to foment a riot.

A lengthy federal trial in Chicago was a judicial "circus," with the defendants and their supporters seeking to disrupt the trial by shouting, cursing, and other wild behavior. Insults were frequently hurled at the prosecution and the judge.

In the end, the jury acquitted all seven of the more serious conspiracy charge, but found five defendants—all but Froines and Weiner—guilty of crossing state lines to incite a riot. Maximum sentences of five years in prison and fines of $5,000 were imposed. In addition, the defendants were ordered to pay a portion of the court costs, which may run as high as $50,000. At this writing, all five are free on bail pending appeals.

As in all political trials, the criminal merits of the case, such as they were, became lost in the shuffle of other issues. One issue was the disruptive tactics of the defendants. Stating that they would not get a fair trial, the defendants sought to make it as difficult as possible. Their activities received a severe setback at the close of the trial. The Supreme Court, ruling in another case where similar disruptive behavior had taken place, stated that a trial judge could take any action, including binding and gagging the defendant or trying him in absentia, if it was necessary to protect the integrity of the court proceedings.

Another issue involved the actions of Federal Judge Julius Hoffman. At the outset of the five-month-long trial, he jailed two lawyers for failing to appear in court, even though they had only helped to prepare the defense. He barred such potentially important defense witnesses as former Attorney General Ramsey Clark and Civil Rights Leader Ralph Abernathy. Before the jury, he praised prosecutor Thomas Aquinas Foran and put down defense attorney Leonard Weinglass by consistently mispronouncing his name. Finally, at the conclusion of the trial, Judge Hoffman handed out heavy contempt of court sentences against the defendants and their attorneys. These sentences ranged from two months and 18 days for Lee Weiner to 29 months and 16 days for David Dellinger. Chief defense attorney William Kunstler received four years and 13 days for contempt. Some legal experts sharply criticized these contempt sentences, for they occurred without any trial before an impartial judge or jury.

The trial occurred amidst massive publicity with the American people sharply divided in defense of the participants. Vice President Spiro Agnew termed the defendants "anarchists and social misfits" and added: "Fortunately for America the system proved equal to the challenge. That jury came in with an American result." New York Mayor John Lindsay saw things differently. "All of us, I think, see in that trial a tawdry parody of our judicial system," he said. "When a trial becomes fundamentally an examination of political acts and beliefs then guilt or innocence becomes almost irrelevant." After the verdict, protest demonstrations, some of them violent, occurred in various cities and universities.

The trial of the Chicago Seven is not an isolated case. Numerous leaders of the Black Panther Party face trial on a variety of charges including murder of policemen. In mid-1970, indictments were returned against thirteen leaders of the Weathermen, the militant wing of the Students for a Democratic Society.

How can a judicial system which upheld the dissents of such people as Charles Baker, Linda Brown, and Walter Gobitis also perpetrate such dubious convictions as those of Eugene Debs, Sacco and Vanzetti, Alger Hiss, and the Chicago Seven? How can the same judicial system both honor dissent and repress it?

In his book, *Concerning Dissent and Civil Disobedience*, former Supreme Court Justice Abe Fortas emphasized the right of government to protect both itself and the people from harm or injury. He said government may repress any *action* which could bring such harm. One of the difficult tasks of the Court, he added, is to mark the fine line which separates free speech and symbolic speech from actions which are injurious to people or a threat to government. To give one example, is a man criticizing the government before a large crowd of people engaging in free speech or inciting a riot, if a riot occurs? As long as the need to differentiate between words and actions exists, the political trial is sure to occur.

It is perhaps not stretching Justice Fortas' views too far to suggest that the seeming paradox of American justice both protecting and repressing dissenters exists because of the courts' role in differentiating valid from invalid laws, words from action, civil disobedience from lawlessness.

It is possible to make another distinction. Most of the successful dissents described in the last chapter, such as that of the Gobitis family, and Linda Brown were initiated in the courts. No attempts were made to foment revolution, organize street protests, strike, or boycott. The dissent was expressed through the courts in a legal way. And the dissenters were successful in at least getting a hearing.

On the other hand, when the expression of dissent takes to the streets with violence, in strikes, boycotts and massive marches and demonstrations, it runs the risk of being met with repressive action.

Chapter 9
Disunity Among
Dissenters

ANOTHER PATTERN to dissent is only indirectly related to
either the issues or the forms of dissent. Dissenters have
tended to splinter into fractional groups. Unity has always been a scarce commodity among dissenters.

The American system of dissent probably makes this
inevitable. There are many ways of expressing dissent.
It is perhaps impossible for the dissenters not to argue
over the most effective form of dissent. Some urge publication, speech making, and public education. Others
believe political activity will work best. Another group
wants to test their cause in the courts. Some conclude
that the whole political and economic system is bad and
urge violence and revolution. Unable to convince other
dissenters to their views, the body of people who basically agree on the same issue break up into separate, often
rival groups.

Success also leads to division. Unity comes easy when the dissenters are "voices in the wilderness" trying to convince the "establishment" that an evil exists which ought to be corrected. Then the dissenters begin to win more people to their side. Politicians and public figures embrace their point of view. Some laws are passed, some organizations take remedial action. The initial success pleases a few of the dissenters. With more success, still more dissenters are satisfied. Ardor for the cause diminishes. Some radical dissenters take a more conservative position. Those dissenters who are not satisfied with the progress move further to the left, advocating more vigorous and extreme means of expressing dissent. The conservatives and radicals both fight for the allegiance of the moderates not committed to either position.

The long struggle of the labor movement is an excellent example of the dangers of disunity. Since colonial times, the American workingman has wanted essentially the same things: shorter hours, higher pay, better and safer working conditions, recognition of his union, security in his job and in his earnings, and enough voice in management to achieve these goals.

Yet unity of aspiration is the only unity labor has ever had. Workingmen have never been able to get together to offer a unified front that would effectively use the power of their numbers against the monetary power of management. Today the AFL-CIO (American Federation of Labor and Congress of Industrial Organizations) is plagued with dissension and disunity. Several powerful unions do not belong or are members in name only.

There were (and are) a variety of reasons why unity never came. For one, management, allied for so long with government, tried mightily to keep labor disunited. Management would promote to foreman or other management position the bright young wage earner who showed promise of being a labor leader. Other leaders were arrested, jailed, or harrassed. Management would set up or otherwise encourage rival labor organizations that were more tractable in bargaining over wages. Management would make wage offers calculated to entice a large segment of the union men, thus fostering disunity and breaking the strike. Or, management would remain intractable, offering less wages than before the strike, call out police and troops, and wear down the union men through hardship and attrition.

Certainly until World War I, the nation's economic and political system encouraged disunity among labor. There were a host of labor organizations and political parties built around the labor vote, such as: the Locofocos, Tammany Hall, National Labor Union, Knights of Labor, American Railroad Union, Industrial Workers of the World, Labor Party, Socialist Labor Party, Independent Labor Party, Populist, Socialist, Farmer-Labor, American Workers Party, and several Progressive parties.

Each flourished for a time and garnered a number of adherents. But always several things would happen. A time of prosperity would occur, leading many workers to abandon the organization as unnecessary. Or, "hard times" would occur. Workers would be reduced to such states of poverty that search for employment, any employment, forced them to abandon their union in order to eat. Members of labor parties grew discouraged in their efforts to start a third party, or else one of the major parties adopted their platform.

Labor also dissipated its strength by failing to agree on nearly everything except its aspirations. To this day labor has never been able to agree on the best way to organize a union. The AFL believes in the craft union, that is, pipefitters or bricklayers or carpenters belong to the same union no matter in which industry they work. Thus, all members of an AFL union have a skill in common. The CIO believes that all workers in the same industry should belong to the same union, regardless of the type of work they do or the skills they possess. Thus, the steelworkers, auto workers, rubber workers, and communications workers are members of the CIO. The two types of unions have always squabbled and competed with each other.

Workingmen have long argued over the best way to achieve their aspirations. Some have wanted to work "within the system," that is, to form political parties or infiltrate existing parties so as to use the ballot box to bring about the desired changes. Others have wanted to fight through the courts. Still others have believed in mass protests, seeking to sway public opinion so that there would be a national demand for reform. There were those who believed that only by developing the union strength, by organizing *all* workers could reform occur. Another viewpoint was that labor should forget politics, forget public opinion, and concentrate on specific goals of shorter hours, higher wages, etc., from individual companies and factories. Thus, reform would occur piecemeal. Finally, there were those radicals who believed the entire system must be changed. Capitalism was incapable of reform. Socialism was the only answer. When the New Deal administration of Franklin D. Roosevelt adopted most of the socialist platform, some socialists turned to the right while others became Communist, insisting that the only answer was a proletarian, Russian-style revolution.

The in-fighting that has occurred in the name of these various techniques of dissent is staggering. Much of it centered around the AFL, founded in 1881. It was the first, and, for fifty years, the only enduring national labor organization. A craft union, it assumed a moderate position, defending all laboring men in their battles with management and government, yet insisting upon achieving specific goals in terms of hours, wages, and working conditions. It had no strong rival until the CIO was founded in the 1930s.

During that time, repeated efforts were made to "capture" the AFL for socialism or other radical causes. Debs tried and so did Daniel de Leon. De Leon was a direct descendant of the discoverer of Florida. He immigrated to the United States in 1872, a linguist and a scholar. Devoted to the labor movement, he gradually evolved into a radical socialist believing in the revolutionary overthrow of capitalism. "Nothing short of socialism" was his slogan.

137

De Leon tried to control a number of organizations, such as the Knights of Labor and the Socialist Labor Party, and to use them to achieve his goals. All failed. Then, in the 1890s, he made a strong effort to win the AFL to his cause. Samuel Gompers, the head of the AFL, was not unfriendly to socialism. He corresponded with leading socialists in Europe and regularly castigated capitalism for its faults. But he could never quite become a socialist, feeling it was too visionary. He believed in "simple unionism," that is, organizing craft unions and struggling to achieve specific goals.

When De Leon failed in his effort to turn the AFL to radical socialism, he immediately turned into a divisive force, terming the AFL leaders "labor fakers," or "agents of the capitalists inside the trade union" and "traitors to the cause of labor." He declared some AFL leaders "ignorant," others "corrupt," and still others "unfit for leadership." Needless to say, De Leon also excoriated socialists who did not agree with his program.

Disagreeing over methods of expressing dissent, labor splintered into rival groups. Faced with success—management found it relatively easy to settle with the skilled workers of the AFL—labor further splintered into conservatives, moderates, and radicals.

Negro dissent in America is perhaps less united than ever before. Each succeeding wave of radicalism has tended to move former radicals to a more conservative position. The NAACP is considered a rather conservative organization today. Advocates of Black Power are at best moderates. Negro dissent is thus divided over

138

the best methods of expressing dissent, opinions ranging from the "Uncle Tomism" of Booker T. Washington to the violent revolutionary program of the Panthers. And, at least in part, the dissension among the dissenters is a product of the very success of past efforts.

The same pattern can be witnessed in today's peace movement. Both disunity and self-radicalization has occurred because of disagreements over the forms of dissent and the success of the movement. There is a whole spectrum of opinion, including pacifists who are against all war and pacifists who are against particular wars, those who support the gradual end of the war along the lines being attempted by President Nixon, those who want an immediate end to the war but seek to use legal and political means to achieve it, those who wish to continue the street confrontation and public protest, and those who believe only violent revolution is the answer.

Often within a very short time, the dissenters spread into a spectrum of opinion ranging from conservative to radical. In the case of long-term dissent, such as the labor and civil rights movements, new waves of radicalism appear frequently, leading the movement to the left and spreading dissension.

Up to the present, every dissent movement in American history has been captured by those advocating moderate forms of dissent and the achievement of specific goals. Conservatives tend to drift away from the movement. The radicals usually become victims of what they consider repression; their leaders end up in jail or are otherwise eliminated.

Chapter 10
What is Different Today?

Is THERE anything different about the expression of dissent today?

As we have seen, dissent has always been plentiful in America. Yet, many Americans, perhaps a majority, feel that there is *more* dissent today than ever before. It is a notion worth pursuing.

Granted, there is a great deal of dissent in America today, but it is difficult to label it an exceptional period when one considers the massive peace movement of the Civil War, the labor turmoil and picket line massacres of the last half of the nineteenth century, the bread lines and strife of the 1930s.

Today's dissent *seems* to be greater because it follows a thirty-year period in which dissent was minimal. World War II, as mentioned previously, was the only war in American history that did not produce much dissent, after the U.S. declared war. The Japanese attack and the condemnation of Hitler united the American people for four years as never before in our history.

The quarter century from the end of World War II in 1945 to 1970 witnessed two periods which tended to repress dissent. First came the Cold War. America reacted to the threat of Communist imperialism with military preparedness, the Korean War, and an international program of foreign aid to non-Communist countries. At home, America launched an era of Communist witchhunts. A wide variety of dissent was silenced or driven underground after being labeled communistic or socialistic.

The 1960s, which began with the election of John F. Kennedy and his call for an emotional commitment to America, were one of the high points of liberalism in America. The militant anti-communism of the 1940s and 1950s resulted in the war in Vietnam, but in most domestic areas liberalism was in full bloom. Thus, today's dissent only *seems* greater because there has been relatively less of it for a rather long time.

True, conservatives became dissenters during the liberal 1960s. Conservatives, some advocating extremism, nominated Barry Goldwater for President in 1964. But one of the hallmarks of the conservative is simply that he makes less noise. Because so much of the dissent in the 1960s was from conservatives, it made less impression on the public.

A major difference in dissent today is the age of the dissenters. That army of non-violent protesters who

142

marched through the streets singing "We Shall Overcome" and sat in restaurants and public places demanding to be served and accepting arrest when they were not, were mostly people in their teens and twenties. Most of today's dissent about peace, pollution, and other issues occurs in high schools and universities.

Dissent by students and young people simply did not happen very often in the past. Universities were a place of learning. The dissent that occurred there was in the realm of ideas. Students themselves were seldom found on the picket line or in a street protest. For them to *lead* either was unheard of. Generations of Americans prided themselves that United States universities were not seats of rioting, protest, and dissent as were those of Europe and Asia.

Why has this changed? Why are the young dissenting? Statistically there are simply more young people than any other age group. They are also better educated. More than half the high school graduates are going to college. Young people have more knowledge and awareness than in former generations. And colleges concentrate young people in small areas. They have a built-in assembly point where dissent can be cultivated and nourished.

Today's young people are different and their world is different, and they seek to give expression to those differences at every opportunity, in dress, hair styles, music, art, literature, morals, attitudes, and much more.

Perhaps every generation has rebelled against its parents, but probably no generation ever had so much to rebel about. Technological and biological change is occurring with breathtaking rapidity. What is a certainty today may not exist tomorrow. And this applies to the world. Through a combination of overpopulation and pollution—let alone nuclear accident—this could be the last or next-to-last generation. Knowledgeable people have predicted that this planet may be uninhabitable by the year 2,000 or close to it. This may be an exaggeration—but then again it may not.

Suffice it to say that young people are dissenting about the world they have inherited. They are dissenting about the ideas, attitudes, and practices of the older generation which have led the world to this state. And this dissent by the young is filled with impatience, partly because impatience is the hallmark of the young, but mostly because in a rapidly changing world there isn't much time. The worldwide problems of overpopulation, pollution, and war must be solved in decades, not in centuries. The leisurely pace of dissent in the past has been greatly accelerated. Technology is widening the cultural gap or the sociological gap or the psychological gap. Man himself must change and quickly. Today's dissenters are more aware of this than in any previous generation.

Are the issues of dissent different today? Some are and some are not. The economic issues which so dominated dissent in the past have lost importance. There are still isolated struggles, such as among migratory workers, but organized labor has largely won its battles. Strikes and labor disputes occur, of course, but they are largely ritualistic affairs between powerful industries and labor

144

unions. The biggest problem in labor relations today is among unorganized service workers and government employees. Economic dissent centers more today on the elimination of poverty in a land of plenty and on upgrading the quality of products made and work performed in America. Perhaps incredibly, socialism and communism are still being advocated by some dissenters today, the Black Panthers, for example. But the problems and quality of life in many socialistic and communistic countries have tended to diminish enthusiasm for these economic "utopias."

Religion is still an issue of dissent. Many of the leading religious sects are re-examining themselves and are experiencing dissent among their members. Dissent in the Catholic Church, for example, is pronounced over such issues as birth control, Papal authority, and celibacy for priests and nuns.

Race remains an issue of dissent in America, as it always has been. Black people have in recent years destroyed much of the legal basis for segregation and discrimination. The problem now is to achieve practical equality in education, employment, housing, health, and other areas. Even more difficult is ending the private discrimination against Negroes by changing the racial attitudes of both races.

Women's liberation is still an issue, but, like the race question, it is a problem of winning practical equality.

Peace is a greater issue than ever before. The War in Indochina is the least popular in which the United States has ever been engaged. Much of the dissent concerns the morality and waste of the war. But at least part of the dissent concerns the futility of war in a nuclear age. Many of the dissenters are saying that it is past time that mankind learned some other solution to international disputes than warfare.

The newest issue and perhaps the most important might be called *environment*. This includes pollution of the air and water, destruction of nature, and over-population. Environment also includes a somewhat amorphous and abstract dissent over the quality of American life, in which dissenters are objecting to the emphasis upon wealth and material possessions, the search for technological advancement, the impersonality of a computerized society, dishonesty, hypocrisy, and "phoniness" among American people.

What of the forms of dissent. Are they different? No, but they are used differently. There is a great deal of much-publicized violence, but overall there is probably less violence than at various times in the past. The deaths on college campuses and other scenes of protest, regrettable as they are, pale before the massacres on picket lines in the past or the thousands of deaths in lynchings in the South. Conversely, examination of past dissent reveals little to rival the non-violent protests of the sit-in era of the Negro Revolution or the massive and orderly peace marches in Washington and other cities.

There are several reasons for the increased emphasis upon massive, visual protests. Television, as discussed in Chapter 5, tends to encourage these forms of dissent. Also, it is much easier for dissenters to assemble. Young people are already assembled in schools and universities. Our mobile society makes it easy to travel across the country to attend a protest rally. Also, the dominant issues of race, peace, and environment lend themselves more to mass protest. Besides, these methods have a proven record of success in the fields of civil rights and peace.

There is one more major difference in today's dissent, which has not previously been referred to in this book. Some of today's dissent seeks non-specific goals. The American system, indeed any government, can deal only with the specific. The government can pass a law or adopt a policy. Individuals or institutions can begin a program or conceive a policy. Dissent in the past recognized this. Labor fought for higher wages and specific benefits. Even radical socialists and communists offered a specific program of revolution to change the economic and political system. Negroes fought for integration of public accommodations, better schools, more jobs, the vote, and other specific goals. Women wanted the vote and an end to job discrimination. Jehovah's Witnesses wanted the right not to salute the flag.

In short, virtually all dissent of the past was aimed at achieving a specific goal which was within the power of American government or institutions to grant. Much, perhaps most, of today's dissent is similar. Dissenters want an end to the war in Indochina, universities that are more democratic and responsive, greater public expenditures for housing, health, education, and other urban problems, greater impartiality on the part of police, an end to the pollution of air and water. These are specific goals. It is within the capability of the system to do something about them.

But there is also a great deal of dissent which carries with it no specific program of remedial action. Militant elements among women and Negroes, when their demands are reduced to the simplest terms, want the rest of Americans to start thinking and acting differently toward them so that inequality that stems from private discrimination can be ended. It is very difficult, however, to think of a law which Congress might pass or a policy which an institution might adopt which would bring about a very rapid alteration of what goes on in the hearts of men.

Some dissenters talk about the alienation of youth. It is hard to think of specific public actions, other than aging, which will do very much to bridge the generation gap. There is dissent about America's emphasis on progress, money, and material possessions. A person might agree most ardently, but it is difficult to think of a program to alter these attitudes. A common theme of dissenters is that Americans are hypocritical, professing peace while soldiers wage war and bragging about the Bill of Rights while police club protesters. A great deal could be done about the war and the clubbings, but the hypocrisy poses a far more difficult problem.

The growth of non-specific dissent may stem from the age of the dissenters and the idealism of youth. Or, it may be from lack of familiarity with the mechanism of the American system. Or, this dissent may be simple hooliganism, kicking society when it is down and shows open wounds. Whatever the reason, a serious problem results.

Non-specific goals dealing with private attitudes and actions of Americans can be corrected only with time and education. The United States has made many attempts to legislate morals, attitudes, and conduct, and the results have been generally disastrous. Prohibition was one. Saluting the flag and being patriotic was another. Teaching the literal interpretation of the Bible was still another. America has hopefully learned from some rather bitter experiences that government cannot legislate what goes on in the mind and heart of a man.

This is not to say that non-specific dissent is bad. Citing shortcomings in the attitudes of man as an individual and society as a whole has been the province of clergymen, for example, for thousands of years. As a means of education and evolutionary change, it is highly to be recommended. But to urge violent revolution or government action in pursuit of a non-specific goal, no matter how desirable, is to rush in where angels just won't go.

What will happen to today's dissent and dissenters? With one exception it is impossible to predict. Perhaps today's bombers and revolutionaries will carry the day where those who went before failed. Perhaps dissent and dissension will grow until all unity is destroyed and the United States becomes the quarreling, noisy "noyau" described by Robert Ardrey in *The Territorial Imperative*, rather than a nation unified in common goals and defense. Perhaps the dissenters will lose and this planet

149

will become uninhabitable within a generation or two, or perhaps there will be nuclear holocaust making the plot of the movie "Planet of the Apes" prophetic.

But it must be said that there is also evidence that the American system of dissent is still functioning. Revolutionaries and rioters are still feeling the heavy hand of repression. Presidents and politicians are responding to the petitions and protests of dissenters. The vote at the national level has been extended to eighteen-year-olds. Established political parties are seeking ways to garner votes of dissenters. Industrialists such as Henry Ford II are launching programs of public service to make capitalism more responsive to issues of the day and are saying that making a profit is not the sole task of industry. Universities are admitting students to boards of trustees. Yes, there is evidence, as this book has tried to show, that the system of dissent is alive and well.

The one prediction that can be made is that today's dissenters, many of whom are young, will grow older. In twenty years, America will have an awful lot of middle-aged people and in forty years an awful lot of old people. In fact, the tremendous numbers of teens and twenties that exist today are likely to remain numerically dominant for the next half century. The birthrate in the United States has dropped sharply. Between 1960 and 1969, the growth rate of the U. S. population was cut almost in half, from 1.5 per cent to 0.8 per cent. The year 1968 saw the lowest birthrate in history. If this trend continues or even stabilizes at the present lower level, the United States will arrive at a situation essentially opposite to today's. By the year 2,000, the numerically largest group in the population will be the elderly. Young people will be a minority.

That leads to some questions: will the United States still be youth-conscious in the year 2000? Will the effects of aging turn today's dissenters and radicals into a more conservative, less adventuresome, but still numerically dominant group? Will this tremendous body of middle-aged and older people be faced with the problems of rebellious, dissenting youth?

If history has any relevance to the future, it seems likely that today's dissenters will face a new generation of dissenters. But how? In fear and distrust or with open minds and open hearts?

Selected Reading

Bell, David, editor, *Confrontation; the Student Rebellion and the Universities.* Basic Books, New York, 1969.

Bender, Edward J., *Turmoil on the Campus.* H. W. Wilson and Company, New York, 1970.

Cantor, Norman F., *The Age of Protest; Dissent and Rebellion in the Twentieth Century.* Hawthorn Books, New York, 1969.

Douglas, William O., *Points of Rebellion.* Random House, New York, 1970.

Fortas, Abe, *Concerning Dissent and Civil Obedience.* The World Publishing Co., Cleveland, Ohio, 1968.

Gray, Wood, *The Hidden Civil War, The Story of the Copperheads.* The Viking Press, New York, 1942.

Kane, Frank, editor, *Voices of Dissent.* Prentice-Hall, Englewood Cliffs, New Jersey, 1970.

Lens, Sidney, *Radicalism in America.* Thomas Y. Crowell Co., New York, 1966.

Libarle, Marc and Tom Seligson, editors, *The High*

School Revolutionaries. Random House, New York, 1970.

Liston, Robert A., *Politics from Precinct to President.* Delacorte Press, New York, 1968.

Liston, Robert A., *Tides of Justice.* Delacorte Press, New York, 1968.

Morison, Samuel Eliot, Frederick Merk, and Frank Freidel, *Dissent in Three American Wars.* Harvard University Press, Cambridge, Mass., 1970.

Index

About the Author

ROBERT LISTON was born in Youngstown, Ohio. He graduated from Hiram College, Hiram, Ohio, with a major in history and political science. Mr. Liston began writing for magazines in 1957 and turned to free lance work in 1964. *School Library Journal* selected his book, DOWNTOWN: *Our Challenging Urban Problems* (Delacourte Press) as one of the best books for young people published in 1968, and Robert Liston takes pride in this kind of recognition.